The *Sail* Book of

Commonsense Cruising

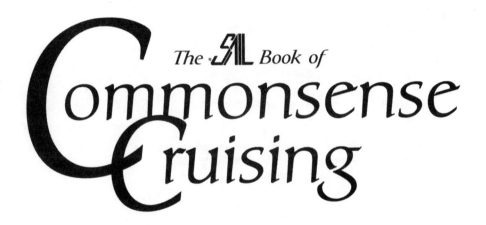

The **SAIL** *Book of*
Commonsense Cruising

Edited by Patience Wales
Illustrations by Kim Downing

ADLARD COLES NAUTICAL
London

Published 2001 by Adlard Coles Nautical
an imprint of A & C Black (Publishers) Ltd
35 Bedford Row, London WC1R 4JH
www.adlardcoles.co.uk

With acknowledgement to the staff of SAIL Magazine

Photos by the authors unless otherwise indicated.

ISBN 0-7136-6082-1

A CIP catalogue record for this book is available from the
British Library.

Note: While all reasonable care has been taken in the publication
of this book, the publisher takes no responsibility for the use of
the methods or products described in the book.

Printed and bound in the United States of America

CONTENTS

I. TECHNIQUES:

II. BOAT CARE:

FOREWORD

What is commonsense cruising? It's really just another way to describe seamanship, a way of viewing the surrounding water and sky with a sailor's eye and then coping efficiently with what you see and hear and smell. Commonsense cruising involves basic boat-handling, crisis management, people management, weather awareness, money awareness, and the tempering of your life afloat with the judgment that comes from experience.

The problem with experience is that acquiring it takes time. You can't buy it or hurry it or give it short shrift. You can learn from other sailors' experience, however, and avoid making many of the mistakes you would make if you were starting from scratch. What's perhaps best of all about cruising on a small sailing boat is this: Getting there is as much fun as being there, and the experience you gain on the way is never wasted. Cruising is like taking a series of courses in a school with no graduation ceremonies. It involves a lifetime of learning. You never know it all. The two elements your boat is using for propulsion—water and air—are filled with surprises, and you can never stop paying attention to these teachers.

When you arrive in port after hours or days or weeks on your boat you get a new view of the world. Whether you've reached five miles down the lake on a sunny Sunday afternoon or crossed the Atlantic to spend a month cruising Scotland, you become a part of the landscape. You tie up to its docks, you use its water, you spend money in its stores. You haven't come on a tour bus with a tour guide. You are your own tour guide on your own vessel with a custom-designed itinerary.

Although SAIL Magazine extends its pages to cover all kinds of sailing, cruising is its backbone. We are constantly struck by how little fundamental difference there is between coastal cruising and ocean cruising. In the boats there is lots of difference and sometimes in the skill levels of the sailors. But the principle is the same. While you're living onboard the boat you're floating in your own world, and this world includes adventure, seclusion, peacefulness, and the satisfaction of making your own decisions and dealing with the consequences of those decisions.

We bought and published the stories that make up this volume because we believe they open a door to this world of cruising. They constitute a kind of preview, an intellectual viewing of a very physical life. One of the things I've always loved about cruising is its tactility. A landbound person can go days without being truly aware of the weather. With air-conditioning and heating in buildings and cars and houses, and walls all around you, you hardly know that the natural world is out there. On a cruising sailboat you feel the wind and rain and spray; your behavior is directly influenced by weather. It governs your fate. You read the clouds for squalls and the sea bottom to make sure your anchors are set. The sea state is not just a bumpy road; how your boat travels down it can be a matter of life or death. You must be sure you can handle the conditions, you must have the right gear to help you do so, and, most important, you must know how to use this gear. The stories in this book teach by anecdote. Experienced cruisers help you to learn seamanship, to use commonsense in your cruising.

Lin and Larry Pardey, the consummate offshore cruisers, builders of two Lyle Hess–designed cutters, circumnavigators, and writers of cruising and boatbuilding books, discuss the commonsense aspects of everything from light-air sailing to food buying to money matters to stowage to that most nebulous and necessary cruising universal—sleep, and how to get enough of it. Sleep is something that seems obvious before you try to stay in your bunk on a bumpy passage. Without it you can't function well in terms of interrelationships or boat-handling. Because sleep is so important, bunk design needs to be taken into consideration as well as crew attitudes. This is one of many examples in this book where advice is passed on from expert to neophyte, and the new cruiser can learn from the experience of the old salt.

Before you begin cruising you have to settle the life you plan to leave. Julie Palm tells how she and her husband cut the cord holding them to house, jobs, and family. Perhaps your life is not just like theirs, but you'll be able to extrapolate, to use their experience to affect your situation. That's true for much of this book—it's not just an ABC of cruising; it's also a primer of ideas. It will get you started and keep you going.

There's no question that your life changes when you move aboard a sailboat no matter for how long. These changes are all part of Commonsense Cruising. Privacy becomes more a matter of attitude than of space; guests have to be "trained"; which spares you carry can make or break your boat; storing your boat safely and sensibly enlarges your horizons. Being able to adapt to these necessary changes means your life will be filled with new freedoms, freedoms that can open up the world.

Patience Wales
Editor
SAIL Magazine

TECHNIQUES

I

By Lin and Larry Pardey

PLANNING FAIR-WEATHER PASSAGES

Whether you sail the "milk run" or cruise off the beaten path, you can increase your chances for fair-weather passages. Doing your homework is the key. Veteran cruisers Lin and Larry Pardey tell how to choose and use route-planning materials

C hristmas Day, 1993, Durban, South Africa. A dozen passagemakers relax at the "internationals" barbecue. We look out to our boats, and the conversation turns to favorite passages and waypoints and then to the passage that lies just head, the voyage along the infamous Agulhas

Lin and Larry Pardey sailing their 29-foot cutter, Taleisin, **from Africa to the United States**

3

Hints for Using Pilot Charts

If you want to do research involving many pilot charts but save the cost of buying them invididually, the *Atlas of Pilot Charts,* prepared by the National Imagery and Mapping Agency and sold by NOAA, is a bargain. (U.S. pilot charts come only in atlases; BA *Routing Charts* come only individually by month.) The atlases are collections of pilot charts by regions and months.

Long before we set sail, we pore over one of the five regional DMA atlases, studying the wind-speed roses, currents, and tracks of previous storms along with weather synopses for each month. As mentioned, the information is based on the averages from ships' weather reports and must be treated as such. In reality, we know there is little promise that the averages will correspond exactly with the conditions we will encounter. So here are some tricks that we use to hedge our bets for relatively fair-weather passages.
• Instead of looking only at the page for the month we hope to make a particular passage, we also look at the preceding and following months, assuming that weather patterns can change earlier or later than the norm.
• Although the directions indicated by the wind roses are the first item we examine, what most often influences our planning is the smaller diagrams showing cyclone tracks, which we avoid if at all possible. In such areas as the Bay of Bengal or the China Sea, where

cyclones have been known to occur at any time of the year, we look for the month with the lowest risk and for a route outside normal cyclone tracks.
• Some pilot charts and routing charts show storm tracks on the main chart instead of on a separate chartlet. This combined data produces a daunting picture. Referring to the index of storm tracks at the side of the chart and mentally eliminating any tracks other than those of cyclone or hurricane strength gives a more useful picture. It is safe to do this because given enough sea room to heave-to, the majority of well-found cruising boats can, and should be able to, withstand storm-force winds (50 to 55 knots).
• We always check currents, because following a favorable current may add speed and comfort to the voyage.
• The thick red lines running through the main body of each pilot chart indicate the percentage of waves that are 12 feet or more high. As you study the pilot chart, you'll learn that these waves are often generated hundreds of miles from where you'll actually be sailing. So unless high-wave frequencies of 20 percent or more occur where gale frequencies are 3 percent or more, we know that the steadying effect of a cruising boat's sails will mean you can usually discount this wave information. However, when these same swells hit land, they may make an exposed anchorage untenable.

current, past the Cape of Good Hope.

"Be patient," says a second-time South African circumnavigator. "*Ocean Passages for the World* shows February to be the best time of the year for that passage."

Another says, "The pilot chart shows a lot of northeasterlies for February, too." This is the fascinating part of voyaging, gathering the information to plan successful fair-weather passages even off the beaten track.

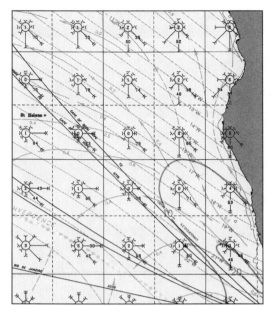

Portion of a U.S. pilot chart. Information includes great-circle routes, gales, wave heights over 12 feet, cyclone tracks, barometric pressure, currents, and visibility as well as winds

After more than 100,000 miles of sailing together, Larry and I have tremendous respect for the old-fashioned manual of route planning, *Ocean Passages for the World (OP)*, published by the British Admiralty (BA) and available from major marine book outlets. The information in *OP* has been compiled from sailing-ship records for over 300 years and from motorized shipping for 100 years. First we look at the "Sailing Ship Routes" section at the back of the book. Then we study all of the information on weather, currents, and warnings in the powered-shipping section for the same geographical areas. The large fold-out maps help us visualize the information.

After determining the months recommended by OP for a particular route and destination, we refer to our pilot charts for those months. Both the U.S. Defense Mapping Agency (DMA) and the BA printing office compile pilot charts (the British call them "routing charts") that show average wind direction and speed, currents, wave heights, and more for each of the world's oceans for each month of the year. These charts are relatively low-priced

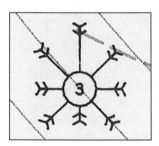

treasures. Since they, like OP, are compiled from centuries of records, and since the averages change very little, one set will last you a voyaging lifetime.

Although British and U.S. charts look slightly different, both contain essentially the same information. We prefer U.S. charts, possibly because we have used them for so long, but also because they show wind roses over coastal areas as well

Wind roses on U.S. pilot charts, one for each 5° square (example above), show distribution of winds in that area based on ships' reports over a considerable period of time. Arrows fly with the wind; length of shaft (measured on a scale, not shown, or a numeral on a shaft) gives percentage of occurrence. Number of feathers gives average force (Beaufort scale). Figure in center is percentage of calms

Formula for Gale Probability

Both the British routing charts and the U.S. pilot charts contain information on the percentage of ships reporting gale-force winds during their passage through each area. The U.S. pilot charts show gale percentages on a separate chartlet, which we find useful in predicting our chances of a gale-free passage. We add up the numbers from each 5-degree square along our intended route. Although these numbers represent percentages, for this purpose we forget about decimals and consider them as simple numbers just as they appear on the chartlet.

Inset from a U.S. pilot chart. Red numbers are gale percentages; zero indicates very infrequent gales

Then we divide this number by the projected number of days we should take to make this passage (we figure about 135 miles per day for *Taleisin*). If the resulting number is less than .6, we find we usually have gale-free sailing. If the number is over 1.1, we have almost always encountered one or two gales along the way.

If the percentage of gales shown in the area nearest our departure port is particularly high, we usually discount this figure about 50 percent because we can delay our departure until we have gale-free weather forecasts for a few days.

As an example, a voyager leaving from the north coast of Portugal in November bound for the Caribbean via the Canaries on a boat that can usually make 120 miles a day would find himself passing across areas with numbers as follows: 7, 2, 2, 1, 0, 0, 0, 0. Added together these total 12. Dividing by the normal passage time of 22 days, the resulting gale-prediction number is .545, which means the passage should be gale-free. The largest number, the 7 percent chance of gales shown right next to the coast of Portugal, can be discounted if the voyager waits for a good forecast.

as sea areas and because their storm-frequency charts are easier to interpret.

The British routing charts contain more-concise information about wind speeds for each direction shown on each wind rose plus the number of ships on which the information is based. Your choice of pilot charts may end up being based as much on availability and price as on merit.

When using pilot charts, remember that the information is based on averages and that weather can be affected by unusual sun-spot activity, volcanic eruptions, el niño occurrences, and even daily temperature fluctuations over large landmasses. So, for instance, where pilot charts show a 80 percent chance for northeast-to-east winds at force 4, you could find unusual conditions, such as the unexpected fresh westerly headwinds encountered by many cruisers bound from Mexico to the Marquesas in 1983 and 1989.

Because pilot charts are compiled from shipping reports, the more frequently traveled an area, the more accurate the information. You should also take into account the disclaimer printed on some pilot charts that historically, ships have avoided areas of bad weather, so that "ships' observations tend to be biased toward good weather conditions—fewer gales and high winds being reported than actually occured." Old pilot-chart and *OP* information is also useful—for example, for sailing-ship routes not used by motorized shipping.

Once you have chosen a general route, more-detailed weather information for cruising near or approaching coastlines can be found in the Sailing Directions published by the BA (72 volumes) or Sailing Directions (Enroute) published by the DMA (37 volumes, covering non-U.S. coastal waters). NOS Coast Pilots (9 volumes) cover U.S. territorial waters.

U.S. *Sailing Directions* have slightly more detailed information about small-boat anchorages. The British *Directions* tend to have more profile diagrams showing approaches from offshore. Both give excellent warnings of potential dangers to shipping. With access to both, we would choose the U.S. publications for U.S. coastal waters and for Central and South America; British for Europe, Africa, and Oceania.

With the increased demand for passagemaking information, some cruising writers have published guides to route planning. We find that there can be problems with their suggestions. At best, the information is provided by a few dozen nonprofessional sailors who make one or two passages across the area. For the most part they choose downwind routes and, like us, avoid traveling during seasons considered less than ideal. Their information is thus sketchy for unusual routes and destinations.

In addition, any guide written by one person will be based on the type of sailing, type of vessel, and type of passages that person enjoys. So unless you are using trade-wind routes, we think it is best to refer first to government publications such as *OP*.

Another source for route planning off the beaten track is the guides to local waters written by local sailors. These guides gain credibility from their authors' familiarity with and frequent cruising in the specific area.

For example, the original spark that led us to choose a southerly route around Australia, to visit Tasmania and then to reach to the Indian Ocean easily in one season, came from Australian cruiser Kevin Lane's guide to anchorages he had visited during a circumnavigation of his homeland. In European waters we've found invaluable information on local weather and currents in Reed's Almanac and the British Royal Cruising Club guides.

As we voyage, commercial fishermen have been an excellent source of information, often in exchange for some beer or fresh bread. We have learned, however, to be selective. Aided by big engines and local knowledge, fishermen working inshore may be willing to lie in anchorages cruising sailors should be terrified to enter at all. If a storm turns their anchorage into a cauldron, fishermen can get out past unlit reefs at night. We've learned to accept their route-planning information and their comments on bottom conditions for anchoring, but to be slightly dubious of their recommendations of unsheltered-looking anchorages.

Veteran delivery skippers can also be a good source of information. When we did our first professional deliveries up the coast of Baja California and later from Florida through the Caribbean, we had to go at times of the year we definitely would not have chosen. By talking with seasoned delivery skippers, we learned about counter currents and wind shifts that we used to advantage.

A more recent addition to our routing sources is the expensive but excellent Admiralty List of Radio Signals, Volume 3—Radio Weather Series. The U.S. equivalent is Worldwide Marine Weather Forecasts. We can pick up on our Sony 2001D receiver many of the shortwave single-sideband broadcasts for areas we plan to cruise. As we listen to the forecasts in the months before we set off, weather patterns become obvious. We have also learned that even during so-called bad seasons, there are often periods of favorable winds. A word of warning: Worldwide radio frequencies were changed in 1991–92. Be sure your radio guide is dated 1992 or later.

Every bit of research we put into finding less-traveled routes as we voyage or deliver boats seems to be rewarded. This was doubly so during our voyage south of Australia. On a previous cruise we had spent six months exploring the Great Barrier Reef on the northeast side of the continent. By going south, we gained the time to explore the remote interior and coasts of Tasmania.

Best of all, by being in place, ready to use the six-week window our research showed would provide good sailing westward across the Southern Bight, we cut out 2,400 miles of hot, humid, often windless sailing through the current- and reef-infested Torres Strait north of Australia. Our reward was a broad reach to the windswept towns of southwest Australia, where wondrous birds fill the beaches, sea life abounds, and foreign voyagers are a once-a-year occurrence.

By Donald Street

GPS AND CHARTS: DANGER AHEAD?

Push-button GPS navigation is wonderfully simple, but not foolproof. Combine GPS error with chart error and you could be surprisingly far from where you think you are

Many sailors believe they know exactly where they are with just one GPS (Global Positioning System) fix. Nothing could be further from the truth. The fact is that many charts in current use, particularly those for the Pacific and the Western Caribbean, were made close to a century ago using now-outdated or inaccurate techniques. Islands and reefs may be out of position by ½ mile or as many as 5 miles. Charted positions from old surveys are usually reasonably correct on latitude but off on longitude.

Recently I gave a hitchhiking sailor a ride, and he stated that according to his GPS the island of Grenada was ½ mile farther west than the chart showed. Two hours later I was talking to a British Naval officer, who said that the Grenada Coast Guard had just installed the latest Royal Navy GPS receiver on their vessel, calibrated by the Royal Navy. Grenada was ⅓ mile farther west than the chart showed.

The following day I was at my good friend Gordon Braithwait's house. We discussed the limitations of GPS, and I pointed out that Grenada's charted position was incorrect. An argument ensued, and we placed his GPS receiver on his lawn and let it run. Half an hour later, according to Gordon's GPS receiver, the island was exactly where it was supposed to be! Three GPS receivers, all different models, obtaining positions on different days, gave a variation of ½ mile. Subsequently I discovered that Grenada was

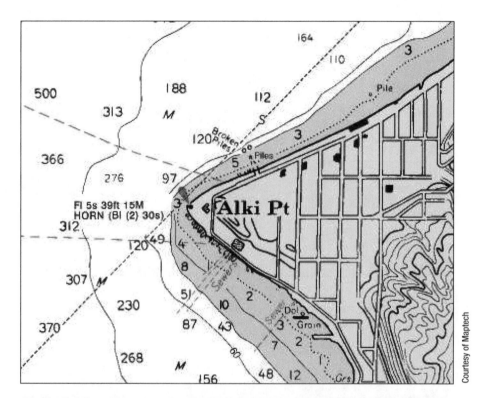

Courtesy of Maptech

Datum shift: Sailors using a chart with an NAD 27 datum (North American Datum of 1927) will find the charted position of Seattle's Alki Point 4.452 seconds (about 100 yards) east of its actual North American Datum 1983 (NAD 83) location. The most up-to-date datums are World Geodetic Survey (WGS) 84 in use by the Defense Mapping Agency (DMA) and the North American Datum (NAD) 83 in use by the National Oceanic and Atmospheric Administration (NOAA); the datums are considered equivalent for charting purposes. Only 54 of NOAA's approximately 1,000 charts have not been converted to NAD 83; about 50 percent of DMA's 3,900 charts are now in WGS 84. If your NOAA chart is old, it may be in NAD 27; many older paper charts that have been reprinted with a datum change will note the offsets in latitude and longitude to convert to NAD 83/WGS 84

indeed charted ½ mile west of its actual position. Here are some more reasons why your chart, your GPS fix, and your boat's actual position may not agree.

The all-important chart datum

A datum is a concept of the shape and size of the earth based on a particular set of calculations or survey. Look on your chart for a datum note or coordinate shift, located under the chart title or in a note in one of the mar-

GPS: Truth and the Position Circle

If you're aware of the potential for GPS error, you've gone a long way toward preventing mishaps. There are 24 satellites in the U.S. Department of Defense's (DOD) Navstar Global Positioning System, each about 11,000 nautical miles above the earth and orbiting twice a day. The larger the number of satellites (up to 12) that a GPS receiver can track and use to compute a position fix, the more accurate the fix.

needed for a three-dimensional (3-D) position, in which the operator doesn't need to enter his elevation. If more than four are tracked, the unit will "overdetermine" or "oversolve" the equation, and the accuracy of the fix will improve. The accuracy does not double if the receiver is tracking, say, eight versus four satellites, but it does increase. Oversolving allows bad ranges to be dropped automatically from the computation.

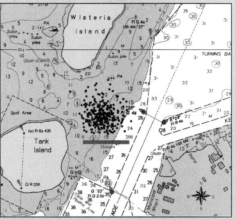

How those satellites are tracked and how their ranges are computed by the receiver's software also contribute to accuracy.

There are other advantages to the unit's being able to track more satellites. A minimum of three satellites are needed for a two-dimensional (2-D) fix; a minimum of four satellites are

GPS makers claim 100-meter accuracy 95 percent of the time—but what does this mean relative to the boat's true position? This plot of fixes obtained over a 24-hour period reveals that any one fix could place the boat's position anywhere in an area 200 meters in diameter. For the other 5 percent of fixes, the indicated position will likely be within a 600-meter circle

gins. If your North American chart doesn't have a datum, the chart is outdated and should not be used for GPS navigation.

If your chart is marked "Datum: WGS 84" (World Geodetic System 1984) or "NAD 83" (North American Datum 1983), you can plot your coordinates from the GPS and pull waypoints safely from the chart. Or the chart may state: "GPS positions may be plotted directly from this chart."

WGS 84 is the default setting for most GPS units. If your chart notes another datum, however, you may be able to reset the GPS receiver to the chart datum and then plot directly onto the chart (the number of datums in GPS units varies from 12 to 100). Check your operating manual to find out if your unit can be reset. It's important to check the datum on each chart you use.

Another possibility is that the datum will be given and an offset—a correction to the geographic positions referred to in the datum—provided to allow GPS positions to be plotted on the chart. These corrections must be made before you plot your GPS position on the chart. In other cases, charts of unknown datum have been cross-checked against charts that have been updated to modern datum, so an offset is provided but no specific datum is noted. In addition, you can find latitude and longitude corrections in Notices to Mariners.

Remember that you must also correct the latitude and longitude of your waypoints before you enter them into the GPS receiver. In well-charted areas calculated to modern datums, the correction factor will be minimal, but in other areas it may be substantial. Always double-check your work. If you do either of these corrections in the wrong direction, you will double the error.

It's always a good idea to proceed with extreme caution. If you're not keeping a good lookout (visual or radar) and checking the depth, you can easily get into trouble. The prudent navigator who uses visual bearings, ranges, radar, and soundings, rather than depending solely on GPS fixes, will increase the odds of staying out of trouble.

Understanding chart error

Considering the difficulty in making charts, you shouldn't be surprised to discover error. Until about 1920, all the basic information for charting was gathered from survey crews in rowboats using a leadline and horizontal sextant angles. Soundings were well placed, but pinnacle rocks were often missed. Compiling the data is a time-consuming job, as the recording must be adjusted for tide height and other factors. And bottoms do change over the years through silting from inlets and rivers, coral growth, and upheaval because of volcanic activity.

After about 1920, powerboats were used to carry the survey crew, but they still relied on hand-thrown lead. After about 1960 the electronic depthsounder came into use, but even with a depthsounder there are limitations. Because of the narrowness of the acoustic beam produced by the transducer, pinnacle rocks or a narrow ridge of rock parallel to the course run by the sounding vessel can be missed.

While much resurveying has been done around major harbors, sometimes little to nothing has been done in outlying areas since the original surveys in the 1920s or even earlier. This fact was impressed on me in 1984, when I was exploring the south coast of Puerto Rico and the Passage Islands. In many cases my 44-foot yawl, *Iolaire*, which draws 7 feet, 3 inches, went hard aground even though the chart showed 10 feet of water.

Ten yeas later I visited the National Oceanic and Atmospheric Administration (NOAA) and noted to my horror that the NOAA 1994 chart of Port Real, Vieques, where *Iolaire* had run aground, was still uncorrected. I had given this information to NOAA in 1984. Knowing the limitations of charting and that NOAA currently has a backlog of 34,000 individual corrections to charts (as well as a shrinking budget), prudent navigators should keep a good safety margin of water under their keels.

By Kim Taylor

EYEBALL NAVIGATION

When you're cruising tropical waters, beauty can mean danger—unmarked reefs and coral heads. Here's how to cruise safely using eyeball navigation and heads-up piloting

The perfect tropical cruising dream of balmy trade winds and crystal-blue water comes with one worrying feature: Sailing among the reefs. Modern electronic-navigation systems, reliably capable of instant position reports to within boatlengths, have taken some of the anxiety out of cruising coral waters, but without accurate, detailed charts (and your GPS corrected to the charts' datum), GPS can offer a false sense of security. Add to this the fact that in tropical waters the maintenance of navigation aids, such as lights, buoys, and beacons, may be indifferent at best, and the need for eyeball navigation and careful piloting takes on great performance.

Understandably, hydrographers have concentrated on charting the waters dictated by commercial and political concerns—often, not the areas of most interest to cruising sailors. A survey every 100 years or so can well keep pace with the growth of coral, but few charts take into account the changes that hurricane-generated swells can make to existing reefs. Often, the scale of a chart is such that it defies precise navigation; not uncommon, particularly in the Pacific, are charts denoting 40 square miles of water as: "Area incompletely surveyed. Many scattered coral heads." Faced with this, your best bet is to develop your skill at eyeball navigation.

Post your boat's lookout at the spreaders (above) to help him or her spot coral heads clearly; polarized sunglasses help

Coral-conning equipment

Up-to-date charts backed up by local information. Begin your reef research with cruising guides, charts, and notices to mariners at the local hydrographic office—and include in your information gathering the old man

16

in the bar who says his grandfather used to take huge schooners through the eye of the area's most infamous coral-reef-pass needle. You'll have to assess your local sources' reliability, but given appropriate weight, local knowledge can be useful. Warning: Don't use black-and-white, photo-copied, or reduced-scale charts—murky reproduction and the lack of color gradations may lead you into danger.

Your boat's compass, a reliable hand-bearing compass, and a working knowledge of piloting skills. With unpredictable tides and current sets in many reef passages, precise route planning is likely impossible; on-the-spot piloting skills are invaluable. Learn how to use transits (both ahead and astern), leading lines, and clearing bearings (Fig. 1).

Figure 1: When entering an anchorage fringed with coral, use range bearings to line up your boat in the middle of the channel and take bearings on landmarks and dangers with a hand-bearing compass during the transit of the pass

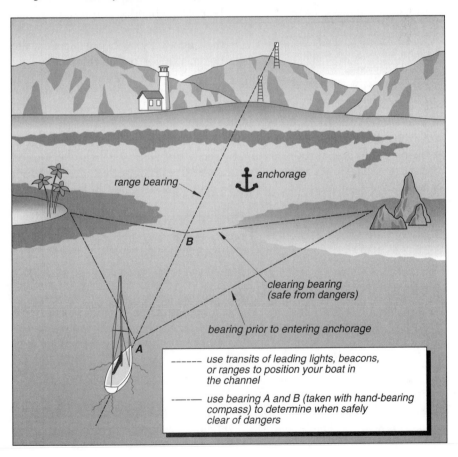

anchorage

range bearing

B

clearing bearing
(safe from dangers)

bearing prior to entering anchorage

A

------ use transits of leading lights, beacons, or ranges to position your boat in the channel

-------- use bearing A and B (taken with hand-bearing compass) to determine when safely clear of dangers

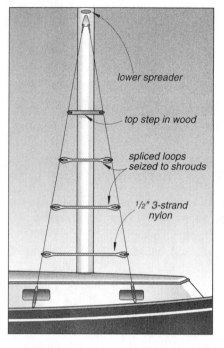

Figure 2: The addition of do-it-yourself ratlines enables the lookout to safely reach a perch on the spreaders

lower spreader

top step in wood

spliced loops seized to shrouds

1/2" 3-strand nylon

At least one good pair of always-alert eyes—preferably more. Equip your boat's lookout with glare-reducing polarized sunglasses and post him or her in an elevated, comfortable spot. Make sure the lookout's roost has easy access; on a doublehanded boat, for example, it's not much help having half the crew enthroned at the top of a 60-foot mast if the engine is out and the skipper has to tack the boat singlehandedly through a narrow reef pass. For visibility purposes, the higher the lookout's perch the better, but for most purposes a spot about 20 feet above the deck, such as on the first set of spreaders, is adequate. A simple set of ratlines (Fig. 2) of 3-strand line is easy to rig and works well.

A depthsounder—provided its limitations are acknowledged. Remember that coral heads, and many reefs, rise vertically from the seabed and thus give little or no warning of danger. If your depthsounder's readout is not visible from the helm, invest in a cockpit repeater. A leadline may prove a useful backup.

Radar. When you're approaching a lee-shore reef with any swell or wind, radar will often pick up the line of breaking surf even if the waves are quite small. Be sure to check your radar's readout against a visible reef before relying on this aid. In normal trade-wind conditions, spume from waves breaking on a reef is visible with the naked eye from at least 2 miles away. Close to, the sound of breaking surf is audible to windward.

Eyeball-navigation techniques

Even when you're armed with the above gear, you should practice piloting in coral—in benign conditions—to develop the following skills.

Make a sketch chart. Keeping a customized route chart topside can be a great help in a shorthanded cockpit. Using info from your official and local sources, prepare a sketch chart (Fig. 3) that shows only the relevant, impor-

Figure 3: To make piloting simpler, use your boat's chart to trace or draw a customized sketch chart detailing the dangers, landmarks, beacons, local-knolwedge tips, and steer-to bearings of each leg; keep the sketch chart at the helm

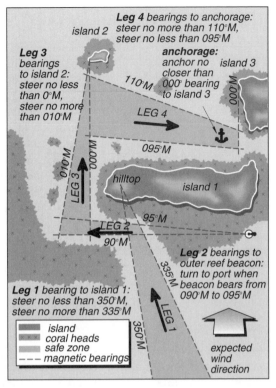

tant information, such as transits, clearing bearings, landmarks, and (assuming no current) courses to steer. Clearly marking the route's "safe zones" will help you stay clear of danger. Also make notations, best written as leg-by-leg instructions, for the route.

When making and using a sketch chart, remember to maintain a healthy skepticism regarding such changeable features as beacons, trees, and buildings. For example, the charted beacon in Figure 3 may, in reality, be missing; even if it is present, the bearing to the hilltop is probably more reliable. Use your sketch chart to plan for possible sailhandling maneuvers, too; in Figure 3 the expected wind direction necessitates at least one gybe—possibly more if the wind shifts. And note that if the wind direction makes the course in a restricted channel (say, on leg 2) directly to windward, it may be wiser to motor.

You can also add cautionary navigation notes to the sketch chart—for example, to remind yourself that where the safe zone is very small you shouldn't rely on a hand-bearing compass, especially if choppy water makes taking an accurate bearing difficult. You can also note the likely direction of current; on leg 4 the flow will probably be either up- or down-channel.

Visibility and timing. Even with crystal-clear water, timing is critical for safe piloting. A dull, overcast day and a glassy sea present the worst water-visibility scenario; a bright sunny day with enough wind to ripple the surface is best. Most often, conditions lie somewhere between. In a changeable situation, it's prudent to wait for better water visibility when approaching a particularly tricky section. For example, the darker water of a cloud's shad-

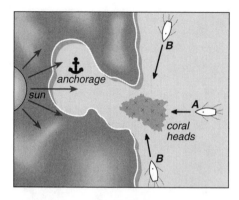

Figure 4: When nearing an anchorage that is up-sun and guarded by coral, make your final approach from an oblique angle to minimize the visibility-reducing effect of the sun's glare on the water's surface

ow can easily be misread as a reef and can lead you to doubt your chart and your position.

The higher the sun, the better the water visibility; the optimum time for piloting is from 1000 to 1400 hours. For journeys of more than four hours, an early departure from a known anchorage at a less-than-ideal time is preferred, thus ensuring arrival at the new, unknown anchorage in the best conditions. Even during the hours of optimum visibility, it's important to plan the time of your approach to keep the sun behind you to minimize glare on the water. Occasionally a tricky arrival, either up-sun or in cloudy conditions, can't be avoided. Minimize the risk by making an oblique approach (Fig. 4).

Conveniently, where the water is continually murky, such as at a river discharge, coral will not grow; usually these areas are reef-free, providing safe access to the anchorage. Beware, however, of recent freshets that have spread the obscured water beyond its usual range.

Judging water color. Most sea beds lighten from "bottomless blue" at about 40 feet to turquoise as the depths grow shallower over sand. Rocks and dead coral are difficult to read, but live coral, nearest the surface, appears brown (if you see small roundels of white, these are the eyes of the reef fish—you are aground). Practice checking your depth estimates against your depthsounder's readout.

Defensive navigation. Piloting safely may include: having the engine ticking over while sailing near tricky bits of reef; keeping your sails handy in case of engine shutdown, favoring the windward side of a reef (in case of engine failure or a windshift) or the more easily visible down-sun side; having your anchor ready to go; marking off your progress on the on-deck sketch chart; and making frequent chart and log updates. Be prepared to stop and re-orient yourself if any aspect of the route does not look right. Make it a habit, when entering a new harbor or reef-strewn area, to verify and make notes on transits, leading lines, and land features for use when departing. Most GPS units allow a "current position" to be stored at the press of a button, thus helping construct a route out (Fig. 5) that does not rely on the chart (steering straight lines between waypoints is necessary.) Also, be

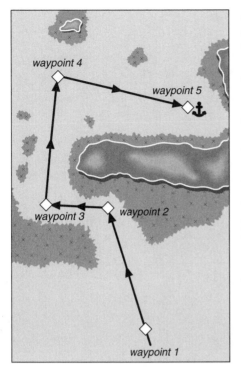

waypoint 4

waypoint 5

waypoint 3   waypoint 2

waypoint 1

Figure 5: Most GPS units have a "current position" button that stores the boat's position at a given moment in waypoint memory; using this feature when entering a reef-strewn area, you can construct a route out that uses the waypoints. Be sure to: number the waypoints in the correct order when going in; steer straight between waypoints; expect and allow for variation between waypoint position and your boat's actual position (don't rely solely on GPS waypoints in tight spots); and use eyeball navigation and a chart

very wary of relying on GPS way-points in tight situations. For partic-ularly difficult areas, reconnais-sance by dinghy and leadline or swimming or a combination of both may be warranted.

Reef-pass piloting

Narrow reef passes are sure to raise the heart rate of even the most laid-back cruiser. If the pass enters a large lagoon and your timing is wrong, you could be facing a strong ebb flow—10 knots or so. Many formulas are avail-able to calculate "slack water" in reef passes, but this can be imprecise. The biggest extratidal influence is the ocean swell that breaks over the lower parts of the barrier reef, raising the water level inside the lagoon and thus increasing the ebb and reducing the flood. Your lookout should assess the conditions before you commit your boat to the pass. The bearing up the pass should be checked against that of the chart to avoid "false" entrances.

An analysis of my own reef-pass scares during five years of cruising among the reefs has shown that all the near-misses resulted from a failure to observe one or several of the guidelines above—and therefore the dan-ger was completely avoidable. Sailing in coral reefs can be a spectacular, rewarding, and safe cruising experience.

By Lin and Larry Pardey

LIGHT-AIR SAIL POWER

Lin and Larry Pardey bring to bear 25 years of experience on the subject of light-weather sailing—which sails to use, how to sail in light zephyrs, the "right" light-air sail

We can't remember a more welcome landfall than Sri Lanka. Our pilot charts had forecast a 14 percent chance of gale winds for at least part of the 2,200-mile passage from Aden, South Yemen, but we'd had breezes so fitful our 24-foot *Seraffyn* sat motionless for hours

The drifter flies to help the main, while Larry looks for signs of breeze

at a time. Instead of averaging 100 miles per day as we usually did, on this passage we averaged only 63.

We were telling Don Windsor, the port captain at Galle, Sri Lanka, about our frustrating 35-day passage. "You did very well," he said. "The seven boats that have come this way since the Suez Canal reopened took 50 to 64 days to make the same passage. There's never much wind out there." He went on to tell us how these sailors had motored, often ignoring the 5- or 6-knot breezes along their way, until they ran out of fuel. Their boats had not been prepared to sail in light winds.

Most cruisers are more concerned with gale tactics than light-air performance. Yet light winds predominate along many cruising routes. If you can keep your boat moving under sail, you'll be able to reach remote destinations instead of determining your route by refueling ports.

Long-distance cruising boats have three special—and major—problems. First, the majority are, to put it bluntly, overweight. Second, they are short of crew power. Last, they usually carry a limited inventory of "luxury" sails, such as light-air headsails. Overcoming these handicaps calls for a combination of design improvements, good sail choice, and sailing tactics.

We've heard dozens of people tell of shortening their mast to go offshore, as if a shorter mast was somehow safer. There is little logic to this unless your boat is tender (not stable enough). A shorter mast means you'll either have to resort to large overlapping sails to get light-weather sail area or, as often happens, install larger fuel tanks to overcome the distance in light-air cruising zones.

Design considerations

Although a boat's potential speed in light air is most accurately calculated by comparing the amount of wetted surface (hull below the waterline) with sail area, we've come up with the following rule of thumb. Divide total displacement (designed weight plus 1,500 pounds per crewperson) by 2,000 pounds to get short tonnage. Divide working sail area (the total of the mainsail and 100 percent of the foretriangle) by the tonnage*. If the resulting figure is much less than about 83 square feet per ton, you'll find it difficult to set the light canvas required to keep your boat moving in light airs. A light-air flyer might carry 110 square feet of working sail area per ton—132 square feet per ton with a 150 percent genoa. Our old *Seraffyn* carried 88 square feet of working sail area per ton, 127 feet with her big genoa. Figures for our current boat, 29-foot, 6-inch *Taleisin,* are similar.

* While the Pardeys' criteria will ensure enough sail area for similar designs in their boat's size range, the optimum values change as a function of size and boat type. Although the high sail area per short ton (2,000 pounds) gives good light-air performance in the examples cited, designers use a sail area-to-wetted surface ratio for light-air performance measurement because frictional drag is most important in these conditions.—Ed.

Taleisin *beam-reaching with the drifter. The sail is attached to the headstay by four jib hanks and can be tacked to work to windward in winds of up to 5 to 7 knots*

A Light-Air Inventory

One of the most obvious places to control the cost of outfitting a boat for local and offshore cruising is in your choice of sails. With a new 100 percent jib for a 9-ton cruising cutter costing around $2,000, it is vital to consider a minimalist approach to a sail wardrobe. Space is definitely another consideration on boats used for offshore voyaging. The following would be our recommendation for sailors who wish to consider their engine as auxiliary, for use in and around marinas rather than for shortening time on offshore passages. In each case the assumption is made that the boat carries approximately 83 square feet or more of working canvas per ton of loaded displacement. These inventories are for hanked-on headsails.

Cutter under 6 tons displacement
1. Triple-stitched mainsail with three sets of reef points
2. Triple-stitched staysail with one set of reef points
3. 100 percent jib with one set of reef points to reef to working-jib size
4. Nylon drifter, 135 to 150 percent of foretriangle

Sloop under 6 tons displacement
1. Triple-stitched mainsail with two sets of reef points
2. Storm trysail
[The area of a reefed mainsail may be too far forward on a sloop to work well either going to windward or lying hove-to; therefore a long-footed trysail may be needed.]
3. 100 to 110 percent jib with a set of reef points

4. Storm jib
[If there is no staysail to serve in strong winds, a storm jib is necessary as a back-up sail on a sloop.]
5. Nylon drifter
First luxury sail: 135 percent 4-ounce genoa with reef points

Cutter over 6 tons displacement
1. Triple-stitched mainsail with two rows of reef points
2. Storm trysail
3. Triple-stitched staysail with two rows of reef points
4. 100 to 110 percent jib with reef points or zipper
[A zippered jib or bonneted jib can work exceptionally well here.]
5. Drifter

Sloop over 6 tons displacement
Same as for sloop under 6 tons except we would make the storm jib blade-size with two sets of reef points
First luxury sail: Dacron #1 genoa
Second luxury sail: spinnaker
If you carry a roller-furling headsail, your inventory should include the same mainsails and trysails as recommended above, a drifter, and a reefable staysail. This way you have a separate, strong, well-shaped jib to use in strong wind conditions. This heavy-weather staysail will not only save wear and tear on your larger roller-furling jib, but also give you the flat cut that works best in storm conditions. Should your furling sail or its gear give problems, you'll have to stay with a sail designed to help you claw off a lee shore. This stay will also give support to your mast should the furler stay ever fail.

The full sections of classic long-keel hulls, plus the inherent momentum of a heavier displacement, are often positive contributions to light-air performance. Fuller-bodied hulls can present less wetted surface for their displacement than do many flat-bottomed, fin-keeled racer/cruisers. The additional weight, if combined with a good spread of canvas, helps keep the boat moving between puffs of wind. So, contrary to popular belief, these older designs, such as 1950s CCA boats, RORC-inspired hulls, and classics like Cape Dorys, often perform better than more contemporary designs in light airs.

Propeller configuration also affects light-air performance. In winds below 10 knots, a day's run can be increased by around 4 percent with a two-blade folding prop as compared with a two-blade fixed prop. Three-blade solid props, although they are more fuel-efficient and possibly smoother running under power, are even more costly in terms of boat speed.

Racers know that a clean bottom is essential for successful light-air performance and choose hard bottom paints that can be scrubbed down before each race. For offshore voyagers, an acceptable compromise is a leaching bottom paint designed to be wiped off by a snorkeler three or four times between haulouts.

A clear deck also helps in light air. A clutter of bicycles, water jugs, spray shields, and dodgers causes wind drag. Also, to handle light-air sails, you will need to move around on the side decks and the foredeck. The clearer these areas are, the easier and safer sail handling will be.

The "right" light-air sail

The "right" light-air sail is easy to set and control and capable of being used all around the wind rose. If light-air sails are difficult to handle, many of us take the cockeyed optimist's approach: "If I wait a bit, the wind will freshen." Meanwhile, we curse the slatting jib or start the engine.

The drifter. After trying a variety of light-wind sails, we've found the most versatile and simple to use is our 540-square-foot nylon drifter. It is cut from 1.2-ounce nylon and is the same size as our #1 genoa, but with a higher clew. It can be set flying (i.e., no hanks) on its own low-stretch Kevlar-cored luff rope, but it also has four jib hanks spaced equally along its luff. Unlike the typical asymmetric cruising spinnaker, this flat-cut sail can be used for going to windward in 4 or 5 knots of apparent wind; we use the hanks to help hold the luff tight. Twenty degrees farther off the wind, we unhank the sail and set it flying. We carry it downwind in up to 15 knots of breeze or until its ¼-inch-diameter sheets start to get skinny.

Unlike spinnakers or cruising chutes, a drifter does not chafe against the headstay in sloppy conditions, nor does it have the same tendency to wrap around the forestay in fluky wind. Our drifter weighs only 15 pounds and can easily be stuffed into a space the size of a 5-gallon pail. There is no reason to fold it, as the most diligent crushing seems to have no effect on a nylon sail.

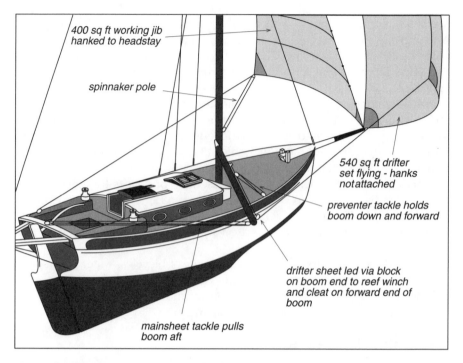

Figure 1: Taleisin's *downwind headsail configuration. The working jib and drifter are easily handled individually. The drifter is set freestanding (no jib hanks) opposite the lapper. With the drifter led to the end of the mainboom and the lapper on the whisker pole, we can run downwind in winds up to 12–14 knots*

In winds above 10 knots we usually run wing-and-wing with our 100 percent lapper set on a whisker pole opposite the mainsail. As the wind drops, we get out the drifter and set it flying to leeward (Fig. 1 and photo, page 25). Its sheet is led to a block seized to the outhaul fitting of the mainsail boom. From there the sheet leads to the jiffy-reefing winch and reefing-pennant cleats at the mast. Since the drifter's sheet and halyard are right at the mast, setting and lowering the sail is a one-person job. To steady the drifter, we push the boom forward and use a preventer tackle to hold it in place. The boom thus works as a drifter pole. Once the drifter is set, we drop the mainsail into the lazyjacks.

Versatility. The two headsails—jib on its pole, drifter on the main-boom—give us almost as much sail area as we'd carry with a symmetrical spinnaker and more than we'd have with an asymmetric chute (Fig. 2), but with much more versatility. If the wind falls light or the sea gets lumpy and the Dacron jib starts to slat or bang, we drop it and use only the drifter. If the wind freshens as we're running wing-and-wing, it's easy to douse the

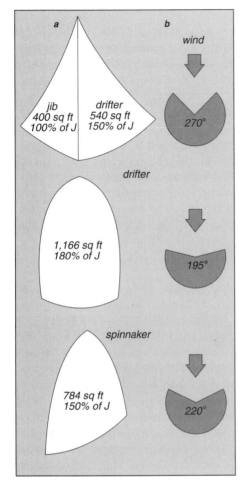

a

jib
400 sq ft
100% of J

drifter
540 sq ft
150% of J

b

wind

270°

drifter

1,166 sq ft
180% of J

195°

spinnaker

784 sq ft
150% of J

220°

Figure 2: Comparative areas (a) for different headsails for a 38-foot boat with an I measurement (hoist) of 40 feet and a J (base of foretriangle) of 18 feet. The drifter-jib combination is not as efficient aerodynamically, but is more manageable and has ample area. (b) Usable range of wind angles for the three headsail types. The shaded areas show the usable angles

larger sail, the drifter. We just hoist the mainsail (ours has no headboard or battens, so it can normally be raised on any point of wind), ease the spinnaker halyard, and gather in the billowing expanse of nylon in the lee of the mainsail. If the wind shifts forward and remains light, we can drop the jib and its whisker pole, sheet in the mainboom and drifter, and set the mainsail, so we're properly canvased for beam-reaching or going to windward later.

Cost. When cost determines your sail choices, the combination of a drifter opposite a 100 percent jib represents the thrifty way to gain sail area downwind. The snuffers often used with a spinnaker or asymmetric chute seem, to us, expensive and bulky. We think they sometimes fail to work properly in the rough conditions found offshore, and worse, they can cause chafe at the head of your sail. By dividing your downwind rig into two headsails, you end up with a drifter than can be handled easily without special containment gear.

By necessity, furling jibs are built to cover a wide range of winds, so sailmakers usually choose heavier fabric than normal and then add a layer of sun-protection cloth along the foot and leech of the sail. Ergo, poor light-air performance. The cost of carrying a light-weather furling genoa, plus the difficulty of changing from one furling headsail to another, could mean you'll just roll up the jib and power.

Mainsails

Mainsails are usually cut from fabric that is too heavy to work well in light breezes, especially in choppy seas. The bang-slat of even the most tightly vanged and prevented mainsail can wake a sound sleeper. When we are trying to cross the seas left over from a 20-knot beam wind with a light wind behind us, we find it best to drop the mainsail and rely completely on quiet nylon chafe-free headsails.

Full-batten mainsails have been suggested as a solution to light-air sailing. But the cost of universal-joint batten cars to make sure the sail goes up and down properly, the common problem of batten-pocket chafe, and the difficulty of raising and lowering the sail at any time other than when you are head-to-wind make us feel this type of mainsail is too expensive for the trade-off of larger roach area, less chance of luffing, and stowing simplicity.

Sailing in light air

Time and again we've felt the magic when light-air sailing tactics turn a dragging night watch marred by slatting sails, a rolling boat, and stagnant position into a gliding swish across a much smoother sea. To keep the boat moving in these light zephyrs it is important to try anything that will keep the sails still and shaped to catch the wind. Inducing a slight heel, either by getting the crew to lounge or sleep on the leeward side or by moving a few water jugs to leeward, will help. Using a vang to hold the mainsail down and out so it doesn't pump the wind out on each swell is important, both on the wind and freed off. Going downwind in very light breezes, it pays to wing the jib out snugly and, if necessary, put a downhaul on the whisker pole to steady it. A smaller 100 percent headsail, which can be held square on the pole, will work better in these conditions than a 150 percent genoa that undulates and curls.

A racing tactic that pays dividends for light-wind cruising is avoiding running dead-downwind unless the breeze is fresh and steady. By reaching up about 20 degrees, even if it is off your rhumb line, you'll keep the boat moving better; you'll cover a little extra ground but will make an overall faster passage. The boat will stay steadier, and the speed gain will be substantial, with less risk of an accidental gybe.

Going upwind on a laden cruising boat in light air, you'll find it pays to keep off the true wind after you tack—to "let it breathe." Instead of pinching right up, let the boat off 5 degrees more than you would in fresher winds. Get the boat moving and trimmed on this easy-breathing course, then slowly work closer to the wind, sheeting the sails in inch by inch. Again, slightly more ground to cover, but a faster passage.

Most other axioms for light-air racing apply to light-air cruising. Ease the halyards and outhaul tension slightly on all sails so there are slight wrinkles but no puckers along the luff or foot. This gives your sails a fuller, more powerful shape. Ease the mainsheet a bit to relieve any weather helm so the rudder can be kept aligned with the keel to cut down on drag. If your boat develops lee helm, as many do under large headsails in light winds, sheet the mainsail in a bit extra. Steer to traverse the seas instead of heading directly into leftover swells or chop, and ease the sheets to keep the boat moving. Over the long distances of a passage, you'll soon make up for any course deviations.

If your windvane is designed to work well in light breezes, you'll keep moving under sail power instead of resorting to the noisy engine. Our system (see photos) has an especially large vane that responds to amazingly light winds. We've found it will keep control as long as there is enough wind to keep the boat moving.

Light-air sailing may be an aquired taste for those who cruise close to home. But for those who eventually visit far-off shores, 60 to 70 miles a day for free can look pretty good. Carrying the right equipment and learning the tactics will make light-air days a rewarding part of your voyage.

II

BOAT CARE

By Bob and Carol Farrington

STITCHES IN TIME

Bob and Carol Farrington tell how to care for and make things with an onboard sewing machine. Dan Haun contributes ten handy sewing hints

A fter six years of cruising both sides of the Atlantic on board *Kitty Grace*, our Goderich 35, we've come to consider a sewing machine an absolute necessity. It has easily paid for itself repairing and restitching our sails and sail covers; it has made us a dodger and shade for our cockpit. Flags, clothing, and upholstery are all products of our faithful servant and Carol's industry.

Our machine is a robust Reads Sailmaker, with a hand crank that Carol uses whenever we are away from shore power. However, any well-built domestic sewing machine will serve you well and can be fitted with a hand crank for use at sea.

Maintenance

The marine environment creates conditions that require special service for a sewing machine. Carol estimates that for every 10 hours of sewing, she spends a half-hour

Moving a sail through a sewing machine can be cumbersome. The sidebar on page 37 provides some hints

Parts of the sewing machine (above):
1. upper thread tension assembly,
2. needle bar thread guide, 3. needle,
4. foot, 5. needle plate, 6. feed dogs,
7. shuttle race assembly

cleaning, oiling (there's an oiling diagram in your machine's instruction book), and just checking the machine. She sprays the entire inside with a silicone spray to keep rust under control; WD40 also works well, but it is a bit messier. She regularly applies sewing-machine oil to all the moving parts of the machine. Caution: Too much oil is almost as bad as no oil, as it holds dirt and lint.

Other parts of the machine are vulnerable to the wear and tear of sewing on heavy materials, especially sails and sail covers. Keep a careful eye on the following (shown in the photographs on this page):

• Keep the shuttle race, located under the needle plate, scrupulously clean and rust-free. Otherwise, it could cause such problems as tangled bobbin thread or abnormally heavy going, or it could even stop the machine.

• If the needle is pulled out of line, it can hit the shuttle hook in the shuttle race assembly and make a tiny burr, which then causes thread to snag or break. Remove the burr with a fine emery cloth.

• Sewing on heavy material requires maximum upper-thread tension. You may need to experiment with the setting of the adjustment nut against the tension spring; test it on fabric of the same type you're sewing. Also, when you are using heavy thread, loosen the thread-tension adjustment screw on the bobbin case a quarter-turn or so.

The feed dogs have sharp edges to push material through the machine; they wear out with use and may need replacement from time to time.

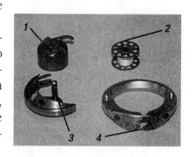

Shuttle race assembly (above):
1. bobbin case, 2. bobbin, 3. shuttle
hook, 4. shuttle race spring

• When the needle hits the needle plate, thread-catching rough spots result. Remove these spots with an emery cloth; eventually you'll need to replace the plate.

• The needle bar thread guide is made from brittle steel and sits in a vul-

Dan Haun's 10 Handy Sewing Hints

I can use a home sewing machine for almost any boat-related project except serious sail work. I've used reference books and advice from a local sailmaker to produce a bimini top with windshield, new sail covers, weather cloths, and a hank-on jib bag. Here's some useful information I've compiled along the way.

1. The important adjustments on your machine are foot tension, bobbin-thread tension, and top-thread tension. Foot tension holds the fabric down when the needle is on the upstroke. If the fabric lifts with the needle, the stitch will be "missed," so increase the tension on tightly woven and heavier fabrics. Bobbin-thread tension is a crude adjustment, but once it is set for the thread, it needs little attention. Top-thread tension is fine-tuned for each fabric; study the stitch and adjust until the stitch is uniform on both sides; don't expect picture-perfect stitches on sailcloth, however. Practice and fine-tune with the fabric you're using for your project.

2. While you're learning, avoid heavyweight, tightly woven fabrics, such as 6-ounce sailcloth or denim. Instead, choose heavy, loosely woven material (such as nylon webbing) or lightweight, tightly woven material (3-ounce sailcloth or spinnaker cloth). Yacht acrylic (such as Sunbrella) is heavyweight (10 ounces) but has an open weave and is well suited to the home machine.

3. Buy needles and thread from mailorder sources, which offer quality Dacron thread and industrial-size needles. I prefer Hemingway and Bartlett thread (size V-69 or V-92) and a size 18

to 20 needle. The extra strength of the V-92 thread makes it my choice for exterior projects, but you'll need a large needle (if you're bending or breaking needles, try a larger size).

4. My machine works best in zigzag mode, with the stitch length set to the maximum and the zigzag width at about three-quarters maximum. Experiment. If you're having problems with straight stitching, try one or all of the following: increase foot tension to the maximum; try a dull needle (slightly flatten and polish the tip on a honing stone); or change to the zipper foot to help keep the fabric in place on the needle's upstroke.

5. Buy the largest pins you can find (I use 1½-inch quilting pins).

6. Avoid snaps from a department store or sewing center; the rings will surely rust. Stick to the marine product.

7. Use Delrin zippers, but protect them from direct sunlight with fabric flaps. The #10 zipper is used for sail covers; the #5 is better suited to interior projects.

8. Hardware-store grommet kits are inexpensive and fine for simple canvas accessories, but use genuine spur grommets for real sail work.

9. For webbing, use the mail-order sources or try an auto-wrecking yard for recycled seatbelts. Use webbing for attachment loops, reinforcement, or finishing raw edges.

10. Practice. Try small projects before tackling a big one. Bags make great starter projects.

—Dan Haun

nerable position. Plan to replace it from time to time (Carol makes her own from stainless-steel seizing wire).

Sewing (and sewing machine) basket

If you're cruising in out-of-the-way places, supplies are, needless to say, hard to find. Carry supplies for sewing projects and spares for the machine. Here's a list we've found useful.

• Machine replacement parts, all available at sewing machine repair centers or through the manufacturer: bobbin case and shuttle race spring (both prone to rust), feed dogs, needle plate, needle bar thread guide
• For hand sewing: a palm, heavy waxed thread, and a selection of needles
• For machine sewing: regular sewing thread; a 1-pound spool of medium-weight, bonded, UV-resistant polyester thread, such as Dabond V-69; plenty of large needles, such as #18/110
• Sailcloth, acrylic canvas (Sunbrella), and clear plastic (for dodger windows)
• Sailmaker's double-sided seaming tape (½-inch wide) to hold fabrics together and prevent "creep" as they pass through the machine
• A roll of sail-repair tape, several yards of 1-inch and 2-inch webbing, and some #2 and #3 grommets and their installation tools
• A small propane or butane torch with a soldering tip to heat-seal the edges of sails and prevent fraying

Troubleshooting

Don't let your machine intimidate you. If you're having problems, always check the simple things first. Is your machine threaded correctly? your thread tangled? the bobbin empty? the needle dull or bent? Learn about your machine and figure out what adjustments help it work properly.

By Tom Wood and Kathy Barron

DELICATE SUBJECTS

Dampness, mold, chafe, and corrosion. These are the enemies of your perishable possessions stored on board. Two liveaboards share their tips—and tips from other cruisers—for prolonging the life of delicate items

T he new hard drive for the computer arrived today," Marilyn said as she slumped into a seat at the yachties' sundowner table. "Second one in two years. The tech in Miami says mold is growing in there from dirty discs."

Four cruisers began replies nearly in unison. Everyone on the patio had stories of expensive losses to dreaded "green mold."

Bob started. "We thought we were saving money by buying a cheap pair of binoculars last year, but now we can't see through them; a fungus etched right into the lens."

"We lost our good 35mm camera and four lenses that way," Kathy chimed in.

I added that we'd lost a bundle in tools and spare rigging parts foolishly stored in the bilge to keep weight low. The parts had been carefully oiled and wrapped in plastic. They had resided down there about a year when we found a mouldering bag of irretrievable rust and green goop.

And the stories went on: books and cruising guides lost to mildew; a black pin mold that grew in "mildew-proof" acrylic dodger and awning fabric. I described my token sports coat that had swung in a hanging locker until it wore clear through to the hanger. A favorite topic for a long time was foul-weather gear and shoes turned into masses of green.

All of us had lost valuable or expensive gear to improper storage. And all

The victims of improper storage: wet, mildewed books; mildewed foul-weather gear; rusted tools. The best solution: insulating the hull, ventilating your storage areas, and making sure the items you store are clean and dry

sadly admitted that most of the loss was preventable given attention to detail and a little extra care with selection of products. The information we shared about the storage of delicate items—papers and documents, pictures, books, clothing and linens, marine fabrics, binoculars, cameras, and entertainment electronics—follows.

Where to put it

No attempt to prevent damage to delicates will be successful if you don't first eliminate such common onboard problems as leaks into lockers. Your boat must also have good ventilation, even on a rainy day. Cutting holes between lockers and removing solid doors will keep air flowing into remote corners. Insulating the hull will help to reduce condensation.

Above all, stored items must be clean. Fungi and molds love to multiply and migrate in dirt and oils. Salt absorbs moisture, providing an environment that is conducive to growth.

Once you've achieved watertight integrity and cleanliness, you can concentrate on the best ways to store individual items. Typically, two methods work best to prevent damage to expensive equipment—either seal moisture out or ventilate the items copiously. Here are some thoughts about specific items.

Papers and documents. Store rare photos and irreplaceable papers ashore. Seal passports, ship's documents, cash, insurance policies, and other important papers in plastic Ziploc-type bags. The heavier ones sold as freezer bags last longest. Personal papers can be laminated to prevent deterioration. It's a good idea to laminate one piece of paper containing all important numbers (passport, Social Security, insurance documents, credit cards, driver's license, and so on) and to store it in your abandon-ship bag.

Pictures. Put developed slides and color prints into plastic holders or sheaths made for this purpose and wrapped individually in tissue. Layer the sheets flat in a watertight plastic box. Add a salt shaker of silica granules to the box. Silica can be purchased in bulk and put into a salt shaker with holes small enough to allow moisture in without spilling the crystals. Heating the shaker in a low oven for 10 minutes drives out the collected moisture.

Books. Paperbacks hold up best; the fabric, cardboard, and glues used in hardcovers hold moisture. Grating, duckboards, and some kinds of plastic matting can provide areas for air to flow under, between, and behind books. Never store books in the bilge or in closed lockers. If books become wet, sun-dry them completely while flipping the pages occasionally.

Clothing and linens. Natural fibers contain oils that promote growth. Select synthetics or blends when possible. Never mix wet or dirty clothing with clean. Off-season clothing and blankets should be washed, thoroughly dried, and then sealed in plastic for long-term storage. Clothing and linens in daily use are best stored folded and stacked loosely in well-ventilated lockers. In clothes lockers isolate metal items, such as chainplates, subject to condensation, as they will leave rust stains. Also, restrain any hanging clothing, as movement of the boat will wear it out. Don't forget about your expensive flags. Wash, dry, fold, and store them in plastic.

Shoes. Shoes made entirely of cloth or plastic are easy to clean and can be simply washed before storage. Leather, on the other hand, requires a careful saddle-soap wash and a coat of shoe wax or polish. Even stored with lots of fresh air, leather shoes turn green.

Wet locker. Since clothing that gets wet and salty must be segregated, a wet locker is a necessity. It should be large enough to hold anything that is salty or damp. The hood and neck area of foul-weather jackets is a usual spot for mildew because hair and facial oils are left there. Wash these often and rinse with fresh water whenever possible. Pipe ventilation into the wet locker from the outside if necessary.

Marine fabrics. One hundred percent acrylic and vinyl fabrics used for awning, dodgers, and other onboard purposes will not mildew. However, dirt, greasy handprints, and enclosed hems hold moisture that sustains various growths. Most common is black pin mold whose stains cannot be removed. Fortunately, dark-colored fabrics hide these stains. Wash with a mild solution of natural soap (not detergent) and a very small quantity of bleach, especially if the fabrics are handled frequently. This treatment is also advised for any synthetic cordage, such as sheets, that have turned green or gray.

Cold storage. Film, vitamins, and prescription drugs will last longer if kept cold. While some people find it troublesome and overly cautious, we also prefer to store our floppy disks in the refrigerator. If these items are kept in airtight plastic boxes, the cold, dry environment protects against mold, mildew, and accidental damage from high temperature. Put copies of the drug prescriptions in the plastic box.

This type of cold storage works best when the cold is constant. It's recommended for mechanical refrigeration but not for iceboxes, whose temperatures fluctuate as the ice melts. When keeping items in cold storage, some precautions are mandatory. Do not allow these items to freeze or come in contact with the holding plate. Never take film or floppies out of the refrigerator and put them directly into the camera or disk drive. Water on the cold object will condense, introducing moisture directly into the hardware. When removing them from the cold box for use, transfer them to an airtight plastic box with a large silica container. Allow the film or floppy to warm up to ambient temperature and to dry completely. Exposed film should be processed immediately. If this is impossible, re-store it in the refrigerator. When developing is available, use the drying process described above.

Binoculars. Purchase rubber-coated (armored) binoculars that are nitrogen filled. The positive pressure and seals that keep this dry, inert gas inside keep growth out and prevent fogging. Binoculars built to military specs will withstand occasional drops in the cockpit but are a bit pricey. Waterproof binoculars should be cleaned often with lots of fresh water.

Cameras. If you use a point-and-shoot camera, buy one of the waterproof or underwater types. Professional underwater cameras such as the Nikons are excellent but very expensive. Otherwise, take the following precaution to avoid damage to regular gear.

Cameras, camcorders, and binoculars need to have a safe haven when not in use. Waterproof, shock-resistant cases manufactured in numerous sizes by Pelican Products come with pre-cut foam that tears out to fit the stored item. In the cockpit, cameras can be protected in an inflatable vinyl bag, such as the Sportpouch made by Basic Designs. A cockpit catch-all for eyeglasses, cameras, and binoculars saves them from falling or being underfoot.

Fungus growth will etch into the coatings on binocular, camera, and camcorder lenses and destroy them forever. Before storing them, clean and dry the case thoroughly. Clean the lenses with lens cleaner and lens tissue. Never use one tissue or lens brush on more than one item, or you may spread spores.

Maintaining cleanliness inside cameras is even more important. Always wash and dry your hands before opening any camera, and wash them again between cameras if you're working with more than one.

Camera bags. Get the padded nylon type, because leather promotes mold.

Entertainment electronics. Most marine electronics are resistant to vibration, sealed against moisture and equipped with a fixed mounting. Home electronics, however, are not. TVs, VCRs, mini stereos, and computers should be mounted on flexible mounts and secured so they won't fall in a seaway. These units should be turned on regularly, because the heat they generate aids in burning off moisture inside. Even then, their life expectancy aboard is shorter than ashore.

How to protect it

Marine bronze and stainless-steel parts enjoy superior resistance to a marine environment. Some very delicate metal items, however, are not readily available in a "marinized" form and require special treatment.

Tools. Such vulnerable tools as the sabre saw, drill, router, and calipers require protective cases. They might all share one large case if they can be separated with some kind of inserts. Hand tools are easy to keep rust-free by cleaning thoroughly after each use with WD40. After cleaning, coat each tool with a fine layer of lanolin and store in a watertight container. Large tools like wire cutters, Nicopress tools, and pipe wrenches can be wrapped in a lanolin-saturated cloth and sealed in plastic. Spare rigging parts should be treated the same way. Do not store them in the bilge.

Sewing machines. Be sure your sewing machine is lashed securely. Clean the machine after each use to remove moisture-absorbing lint. Oiling the bearings is mandatory, and a regular wipe-down of the mechanism with an oil-saturated rag is suggested. Store this oiling cloth in the bottom of the machine. A cover made of wool flannel and a shaker of silica dessicant inside the machine also reduces moisture intrusion.

By Jay C. Knoll

SPARES AND REPAIRS

Which spare parts and "what-if" repair materials should you carry on your boat?
Assessing your boat's systems can help you avoid breakdowns and effect repairs

Nothing is more frustrating than suffering a gear breakdown on your boat and not having the spare parts or materials to fix the problem. Moreover, when your cruising takes you into remote and less-well-supplied areas, you lose the luxury of being able to pick up needed parts from a convenient chandlery. Most important, the difference between full-time cruising and weekend usage translates into greatly increased wear and tear. A year-long cruise, for example, can tax your boat's equipment and systems more than half a dozen years of part-time use would. No wonder many cruisers find that equipment wears out faster than they expected.

But careful thought to the items you include in your spares-and-repairs locker means that not only will you enjoy peace of mind knowing that you can keep systems running, but also that you will avoid the frustration of being harbor-bound while waiting for parts. Finally, you can save money by purchasing your spare parts and repair materials before you leave home.

Spare-parts planning

On *Simple Gifts,* our Crealock 37 cutter, we categorize our spares as either maintenance or repair items. Choosing maintenance gear is relatively simple. Calculate your present annual use of varnish and cleaning supplies and replacement items such as prop zincs and engine belts and filters. Then, for

Maintenance Checklist

We were ghosting along on *Another Horizon,* our Valiant 40, in a light breeze, the drifter flapping as a low swell rolled the air out of it. Time to pole it out. Steve went forward to do the job. After a struggle he returned to the cockpit, muttering about the pole being frozen. Only after massive doses of hot water, various chemicals, and appropriately strong language were we able to free the corroded jaws. Regular application of an anti-seize compound would have prevented the problem, of course. But periodic maintenance is difficult to remember. When was the last time you lubed your winches, for example?

When we decided to go cruising, we were determined to minimize equipment problems by conscientiously carrying out regular maintenance. To help remind us we developed a checklist (see sample, below). First we reviewed the manuals for each piece of equipment, noting both the recommended maintenance steps and the frequency with which they were to be performed. Our boat came with an excellent owner's manual, and we extracted procedures and part numbers from it as well.

Our maintenance checklist includes each piece of equipment, the action to be taken, the frequency and unit of frequency, the type of maintenance, the last time it was carried out and the next time it's scheduled, and a reference to the appropriate manual in case we need to review the procedure. We use an onboard computer to maintain the list; while not strictly necessary, it's handy for keeping the list up to date. The date columns listing the last and next service are entered with the year first and then the month, so when we record the date we last performed the maintenance, the computer can automatically calculate the next date the procedure is due. We can then use the computer to sort the list by the "next" column, which makes it easier to identify the steps due in the current month. We normally check off the list by hand, and when it gets too cluttered or messy we generate another one. Like most cruisers, we still have occasional equipment breakdowns and failures, but after two years of constant cruising we've yet to have a failure due to lack of maintenance.

—Steve Salmon and Tina Olton

Item	Action	Frequency/ unit	Last	Next	Reference
Engine	Change oil	100 hours	1115	1215	Manual #9, pp. 28–29
Engine	Change oil filter	200 hours	1115	1315	
Head	Flush w/vinegar	1 month	01/08	01/09	
Stove	Clean burners	1 month	01/08	01/09	
Prop	Check shaft	6 months	01/05	01/11	Owner's manual, pp. 16–17
Windlass	Check oil	6 months	01/08	02/02	Manual #13
Turnbuckles	Lube and check	1 year	01/04	02/04	Owner's manual, p. 50

full-time cruising, double the quantity. For example, I found that both the increased engine hours and the tropical waters in which we were cruising caused engine zincs to corrode much faster and that no one in the Bahamas carried the particular prop zinc we needed. In addition, our brightwork and fiberglass needed varnishing and waxing more frequently in the tropics.

Predeparture Checklist

On a shakedown cruise along the California coast, we weighed anchor in Newport Harbor for a passage to Marina del Rey. We were motoring out of the channel when the engine-temperature gauge flew into the danger zone. A quick survey in the engine room turned up a clogged raw-water strainer. We knew we had picked up a considerable amount of sea grass while motoring up the channel the day before, but we had forgotten to check the strainer that morning before leaving the anchorage— something we normally do. Our omission made the beginning of the passage momentarily frantic and created a potentially dangerous situation.

Since that incident, we've developed a predeparture list of everything we need to inspect before we raise the anchor or cast off the mooring or dock lines. The list is arranged with items or actions in check-off columns. Each column is used for a single departure; if conditions don't warrant, for example, closing the dorade vents, we put a circle in the column to indicate that it's been checked but not done.

Some steps can be taken the day or night before leaving, such as filling the water and fuel tanks (we know one cruiser who set off on a long passage without water) or entering waypoints in the GPS. Other checks are made just prior to departure: securing the hatches and ports, checking the engine oil and coolant level—and yes, checking the raw-water strainer. A predeparture checklist (see partial sample, below) isn't only for long-distance cruisers; weekend or daysailors will find a predeparture checklist especially handy if their excursions are infrequent.

—Steve Salmon and Tina Olton

- Take seasickness medication
- Check weather forecast

- Empty trash
- Fill water tanks
- Fill fuel tank

- Stow awning
- Replace dodger panels
- Put on windlass cover

- Rig jib and staysail sheets
- Rig preventers
- Rig topping lift
- Adjust backstay

- Secure jerry cans
- Stow fenders
- Secure solar panels
- Close dorade vents

- Check engine oil and coolants
- Check raw-water strainer
- Check shaft log
- Check bilge

- Secure all hatches and ports
- Secure all loose articles
- Be sure cockpit cushions are snapped on

Since space on a cruising boat is limited, try to anticipate what supplies will be available where you will be and carry only those unique to your boat. On our first cruise to the Bahamas we carried enough engine oil and filters for two changes. Two changes later, I could find all the oil I needed, but not enough filters. On our next cruise south, I cut the oil supply down to one change, for emergencies, but I loaded up on filters.

The "What-If" Toolbox

A well-stocked toolbox is your first line of defense in preventing and fixing breakdowns. By organizing your tools into "mini-kits" according to general work areas, you'll be able to find what you need without rummaging. On *Simple Gifts* we carry a mechanical kit (wrenches, sockets, torque wrench, metal chisel, punches, large Vise-Grip pliers, channel-lock pliers, big screwdrivers, hacksaw, battery-powered drill, metal drill bits), an electrical kit (multitester, wire trippers, diagonal cutters, needlenose pliers, soldering iron and solder, connectors, electrical tape), a woodworking kit (hammer, rasps, wood chisels, brace and bit, small plane), and a quick-repair "grab bag" (crescent wrench, large and small straight-head and Phillips-head screwdrivers, tube of sealant, Teflon spray lubricant, electrical tape, rigging tape, medium Vise-Grips, folding knife, and disposable lighter). Check your boat to see if you need metric wrenches and sockets in addition to the standard ASE versions, and consider buying a good set of box wrenches—a must for freeing frozen nuts. Don't forget spares for your tools, especially small, easily broken drill bits and batteries for the multitester.

Crucial spare parts

It's impossible to bring enough spares to cover every eventuality. The cost is prohibitive and so is the stowage. Therefore, you need to combine critical spare parts with a stock of "what-if" materials from which you can fabricate repairs. Start gathering your spare parts and rebuild kits well before your departure date; you may find that local marine stores don't carry certain parts, and you will have to order them from the boatbuilder or manufacturer. Knowing exactly what you need can help save money. For instance, while looking for a rebuild kit for our macerator pump, I found the whole pump on sale for only $5 more than the kit. If the pump fails I can install a replacement and repair the broken one at my leisure.

How do you decide which spares are the crucial ones you shouldn't leave without? Aboard *Simple Gifts* we use a safety/comfort/convenience/likelihood-of-breakdown index. Not really a number, it's more a gut feeling based on past experience with particular parts and the impact their breakdown would have upon our cruising. If a piece of equipment has a poor track record and if its failure would severely limit our ability to sail the boat safely or enjoy ourselves aboard, then we carry the replacement part. Otherwise we depend on our store of "what-if" repair materials to fabricate a fix until we are able to replace the broken item. Our assessment of critical items led us to carry the following spares and "what-if" materials on board at all times:

Engine and charging systems: water pump and impellers; alternator and voltage regulator; head gasket and exhaust riser gasket; heat exchanger

Inflatable dinghy: small substitute dinghy; small "kicker" outboard motor; replacement air valves

Electronics: hand-held backup GPS and VHF; reconditioned autopilot

Systems and rigging: water-pressure pump; extra winch handles

"What-if" repair materials: assorted nuts, bolts, and self-tapping screws; epoxy (WEST System repair packs, and underwater and metal-reinforced epoxy); Superglue; contact cement; piece of inner tube; gasket material (cork and composite material, regular and high-temperature); assorted pieces of plywood and teak; stainless-steel threaded rod; ¼-inch aluminum plate; polyester resin and fiberglass tape; cloth, mat, and woven roving; sealants, corrosion-inhibiting sprays, and marine grease.

General spares

Analyzing your boat's systems will help you decide which other parts you should try to include (these are in the less-than-critical category) in your spares inventory. Here's what we carry aboard *Simple Gifts,* according to area.

Engine: zincs for heat exchanger and prop; oil and fuel filters; alternator belts

Inflatable and outboard motor: Hypalon fabric and adhesive for repair; dinghy pump; spark plugs, prop, and shear pins

Electrical: fuses, circuit breakers, various sizes of wire, bulbs, and connectors

Head: several rebuild kits

Water and fuel: rebuild kits for pressure and foot pumps; rebuild kit and filters for watermaker; hose clamps and barb-to-barb hose joiners; electric fuel pump; various sizes and types of hoses

Sails and canvas: sticky-back Dacron repair tape; sewing palm and sail needles; batten material; grommets, snaps, and setting tool; fabric for sail cover and dodger

Rigging: headstay; rigging tape; wire-rope clamps; short length of chain; sail slides; shackles; halyards and sheets; winch-rebuild kits

Pumps: bilgepump-rebuild kits

Ports and hatches: gaskets and gasket material.

No matter how complete your spare-parts stockpile, your store of repair materials, and your toolbox (see sidebar), you need the knowledge necessary to accomplish repairs—in many places qualified repair people aren't available. I recommend Nigel Calder's *Boatowner's Mechanical and Electrical Manual* as a mandatory addition to your onboard library; take along at least one marine supplier's catalogue and the SAIL *Sailboat Buyers*

Guide for reference and phone numbers to call to order parts. Make sure you carry a detailed service manual for your boat's engine. Consider taking a diesel-engine course from a community college; alternatively, some marine-engine repair companies offer weekend familiarization courses. Arrange for your yard mechanic to brief you on your engine during the annual checkup. Stop in at your local sailmaker and rigger to discuss maintenance questions.

Finally, don't hesitate to ask other cruisers for assistance. There always seems to be someone on a nearby boat who has the expertise, experience, or the right part or fix-it materials, and most times he or she is willing to share it.

By Kathy Mix

STORING YOUR BOAT IN THE TROPICS

It's time to leave your boat behind in southern cruising grounds. Here's how to select a safe berth and how to safeguard your boat and possessions

Two months ago, our marina neighbors here in Florida went home to New Jersey for the summer. "We've been up and down the Intracoastal Waterway every spring and fall for seven years in a row," Mary explained. "This year we're saving ourselves the trip."

Most cruisers prefer to sail in warm, tropical climates. As a result, that's precisely where they are when they decide to leave their boats. Each year hundreds of boats are left in Florida, the Bahamas, the Caribbean, and Mexico while their crews return "home" or sightsee for anywhere from a few days to an entire season.

When you make the decision to leave your boat, two questions immediately come to mind: Where do you leave the boat? How can you be sure it will be waiting safely when you return? In the tropics, other questions arise: How do you deal with the effects of the strong sun? What can you do about the plentiful insects, the heat and humidity, and the variances of the weather? Over the years, my husband, Dave, and I have left our boat in the tropics many times, and we've come up with some answers. We've also discovered that protecting your boat against tropical elements doesn't require hard work or special skills, just some knowledge and thoughtful preparation.

When storing your boat for a short period (a month or two), secure the sails, covers, and all rigging and on-deck hardware

The question of where

If you're cruising the southeast coast of the United States or the Caribbean basin during hurricane season, where to leave your boat is the most important question. Be sure that wherever you choose is well protected. Your best and safest choice is a secure marina or boatyard. In Florida, for example, the St. Johns River and the Okeechobee Waterway are favorites for long-term wet storage, for several reasons. You can leave your boat in fresh water, avoiding marine growth on the bottom, and since both sites are removed from major sailing centers, storage rates are usually reasonable. How far inland you can go may be limited, however, by bridge clearances, and taking your boat inland may require at least one full day of travel. Therefore, you may find a marina closer to the ICW more convenient for a short layup.

Just don't get too close. Avoid any marina that is open to an inlet. Currents in these areas can be fierce, and in the event of a storm, a surge will almost certainly cause damage. Instead, look for narrow or dogleg entrances, sturdy docks, and minimum fetch. There are some excellent candidates tucked

For long-term storage, remove sails and dodger and store belowdeck or ashore. When leaving your boat hauled out, check that neighboring boats don't present a danger to yours and that your boat's jackstands and tie-downs, such as this screw-in-type anchor, can withstand high winds and heavy rain

away in places like Port Salerno's Manatee Pocket or west of the locks on Merritt Island's Barge Canal.

Another alternative for wet storage is one of Florida's numerous private communities. Many offer small enclosed basins, personal attention, and 24-hour security. Cost is sometimes higher than at a boatyard, but you may feel it's worth the extra money.

The haulout alternative

If your boat is of fiberglass or alloy construction, consider hauling it out if you are leaving for several months (a wooden boat is usually best left in the water). When choosing a marina, ask whether you will have AC power available to run a dehumidifier. Check the boatyard's policy on do-it-yourself projects if you plan to paint the bottom when you return.

Inquire about the availability of tie-downs, and make certain your boat will be positioned away from areas used for spray painting or sandblasting. Some boatyards require your mast to be unstepped to reduce windage. This is to prevent toppling and the potential domino effect in high winds.

Before you haul, check the integrity of the jackstands. Always insist that a chain be run between each set of jackstands from side to side to prevent slippage. Don't set your boat under a tree; the shade isn't worth the bird droppings, leaves, twigs, and bugs that will litter your deck.

Protecting against sun

The tropical sun is fierce. Even a light-colored hull and deck will absorb a substantial amount of heat on a bright summer day. Grayed teak or varnished wood will get even hotter. Teak is very durable, but not indestructible; the sun can cause excessive drying that will split even thick planks. Before you leave you will need to protect these surfaces.

If your wood is bare, apply two coats of teak oil with ultraviolet absorbers to seal and protect the grain. Teak decks should be kept under cover, unless you have arranged for a caretaker to wet them down on a regular basis. Overdrying will cause the wood to shrink from the caulking. If your woodwork is varnished, apply at least one extra coat of varnish before you leave (be sure to use an exterior varnish with UV filters). If you're storing your boat for two months or more, shading the wood, especially the horizontal surface, is best.

Sails also need shade. Sunlight is a major cause of degradation in Dacron sailcloth. Even new sail covers may let some sunlight filter through over an extended period of time. Worn, threadbare covers can be very ineffective. To best prolong their life and keep them safe, remove your sails and store them belowdeck or ashore in a storage facility.

If you are storing your sails belowdeck, wash and dry them thoroughly to avoid introducing salt into the boat's interior. Fold and then roll them to minimize the number of creases. If you can, take your sails to a sailmaker for safekeeping and inspection. Sails left rigged for short layups should be lashed securely. Roller-furling sails should be kept from unrolling by wrapping their sheets several times around the sail and then fastening them to a cleat. Furling lines should be brought up taut and tied off, not trusted to a camcleat.

Protecting against insects

Not only does taking your sails down protect them from the sun and wind, it also prevents birds or mud wasps from nesting in the folds. Spiders, too, are experts at hiding in your boat's shaded areas. Both types of insect can invade your boat's interior, so you need to seal off all unused vents and openings. For openings that shouldn't be sealed, such as ventilators, fasten screens or netting securely in place. Stow books and papers in sealed plastic bags to protect them from insects that will feast on the glue. We once stored a box of our boat's books, including a set of sight-reduction tables, in a friend's garage. Six months later they were riddled with tiny holes, and we had to throw them away.

Securing deck gear

For short layups, a wind generator should be left operating only if the unit has a wind brake. But if you'll be gone for more than a month, don't leave your wind generator stopped on deck; when the blades are locked, moisture can cause a spot of rust to form where the ball bearings touch the hardened steel races. When you use the wind generator again, the unit will suffer from drag and vibration; replacing the bearings is the only cure. To be safe, lubricate the wind generator and store it below.

Solar panels should also be removed or covered. They're at high risk of damage from flying debris in big winds. Also, your batteries can be damaged by overcharging (unless you have a regulator that will prevent this from occurring). Remove any deck hardware that is made of plastic; protecting these items will extend their useful life considerably.

Protecting the interior and your possessions

Belowdeck the main element to protect against is moisture. Any leaks, no matter how small, must be found and sealed. Several years ago a hurricane passed just north of where we were berthed, drenching the area with wind-driven rain. The exterior of a neighboring boat that had been stored for the summer wasn't damaged, so the owners didn't bother to return early. When they arrived four weeks later they were shocked. The wind had forced rain in through cracks, and the entire interior of their boat was thickly coated with smelly black mold.

Mildew thrives in a moist environment. To help reduce moisture, get the salt out of your boat's interior. Wash and thoroughly dry foul-weather gear, safety harnesses, and life jackets. Rinse any equipment you bring belowdeck. Slosh fresh water through the bilge, and wipe down all the lockers. If you are leaving your boat where access to fresh water is difficult and you must choose between lashing salt-coated sails on deck or bringing them below, cover them well and leave them topside. The interior of your boat and your possessions will be difficult to restore if mildew gets a foothold.

Clean and completely empty the head, bilge, and shower sump to remove all moisture. Check the owner's manual for specific instructions for the model head you own to determine the recommended cleaning products (some chemicals, such as chlorine and pine oils, will damage rubber or plastic parts). A dehumidifier, if used, should drain into a sink to dispose of water quickly. Lubricate all Y-valves and seacocks, and don't forget to have your holding tank pumped out and to add a deodorant before you leave.

Consider buying a waterproof container in which to store your electronics (add a generous supply of desiccant to absorb moisture). If you have arranged for a caretaker and your electronics are operable, ask the caretaker to run them once a week. This generates internal heat and helps keep the components moisture-free.

Don't leave any open foodstuffs aboard. Seal crackers, cereals, and flour in plastic containers. This not only keeps moisture out, but, in the case of flour, keeps any hatching weevils locked in. If you're going to be away for longer than a month, give away your cake mixes, biscuit mixes, and anything with a rising agent like yeast. Most likely the heat will sap its strength by the time you return.

Protect upholstery and curtains from fading by covering all hatches. Hanging a sacrificial cloth, such as a white sheet, on the inside of windows and ports will also help control the heat. One boat I've seen used solar blankets—an excellent method for reflecting the sun. Lastly, before you go, upset everything. Spread your clothing in nets, stand cushions on end, and lift the floorboards to keep the bilge ventilated. Open all lockers and the icebox. Good air circulation is important in keeping the interior odor-free. Thoughtful preparation will keep your boat protected and ready for you to enjoy when you return.

III

BOAT ISSUES

By John Kettlewell

ONE HULL OR TWO?

In terms of family liveaboard cruising boats, how does a multihull compare to a mono-hull? A cruiser who has owned both compares his two boats

My wife, Leslie, and I have lived aboard a variety of boats for more than 12 years. After owning a series of monohulls—the last one a 37-foot Aage Nielsen–designed double-ender, a traditional heavy-displacement cruising boat—we purchased our first catamaran seven years

I rate our monohull and our multihull equal on anchoring, but the cat's shallow draft makes it a winner in finding secure, shallow anchorages

ago. We'd always been interested in multihulls, but until we bought *Echo*, a 32-foot French cruising cat made of plywood and epoxy, we had difficulty finding one we could afford that was both seaworthy and large enough for cruising. Now that we've had several years of cruising on *Echo*, I thought it would be interesting to compare her with our monohull. I have rated each boat in several categories (listed alphabetically) using a scale of 1 to 10, with 10 the highest rating.

Accommodations

The cat has more room than our 37-footer, but displaces less than half as much fully loaded. The interior accommodates a double cabin with a real double bed (our first), plus a single cabin we've converted to sleep our two children, a galley and a chart area, each 6 feet long, two hanging lockers, a separate head, and loads of storage.

The main saloon, on the bridgedeck between the hulls, has only sitting headroom and no fixed "furniture." We use cushions, pillows, and portable chairs to make it comfortable.

Our last mono had the common layout of settees port and starboard with a gimbaled table between. The galley was U-shaped and spacious compared to others we've seen. One of the biggest differences is that you can sit in the cat's saloon and survey the passing scene through the large ports. The mono's interior was deep, dark, and cool—an asset in the tropics and off-shore. Score: Cat = 9, Mono = 6.

Anchoring

We quickly learned some of the tricks of the catamaran trade as we headed south within days of purchasing our boat. A cat's high freeboard, especially with a bridgedeck cabin, acts just like a sail in high winds—in fact, I can barely hold the anchor rode in conditions in which I would have pulled it right up on our old boat. If an anchor breaks free, we sail away so fast the anchor has trouble resetting.

To prevent most anchoring problems we use a 35-pound CQR, with 50 feet of ⁵⁄₁₆-inch chain and 200 feet of ⅜-inch nylon, for our main anchor. Two FX-23 Fortress anchors with short lengths of chain and plenty of nylon act as second anchors or kedges. We have a small manual Lofrans windlass, which is barely adequate in winds over 20 knots. We often have to motor up on the anchor in difficult situations.

The saving grace at anchor is the ability to lead a bridle to the main rode from the bow of each hull. The bridle eliminates most of the tendency to sail around at anchor. We lead a rode over one bow roller, then attach a line from the other bow equal in length to our boat's beam. With a bridle rigged we ride steadier than most monohulls. During Hurricane Bob, we rode securely in 100-mile-per-hour winds while other boats yawed back and forth wildly. Though the pull is greater, the steady ride seems to help the anchors hold. Score: Cat = 7, Mono = 7.

Docking

Docking can be somewhat problematic on our cat. Our centrally mounted 9.9-horsepower four-stroke outboard provides enough push to go about 5 knots in flat water. We can't steer the outboard, and the prop wash doesn't flow across the rudders. Luckily, we prefer to anchor out most of the time. For those more intent on using slips, I would recommend a cat with a steer-

The cat's windage makes docking it more problematic; the width of a larger cat could make it harder to find a large-enough slip

able outboard or one with twin engines. Some cats with twin inboards are poor performers under sail (especially if they don't have enough sail area), but handle like a dream under power.

The cat's windage can make approaching a dock exciting. It is difficult to get aligned beam-on to a dock that is to windward, as you blow off it faster than you can get a line ashore. Sometimes we have to motor our twin bows right up to the dock, and hold the boat into the wind until the lines are out. When the wind is blowing onto the dock, it is hard not to arrive too quickly—and then it is difficult to leave. A cat will blow sideways at an amazing speed if given the chance. Another problem with cats larger than ours is finding a slip with sufficient width. Our 16-foot beam is rarely a problem. Score: Cat = 6, Mono = 8.

Draft

A great asset, and a boon to safety, is the ability to find shallow, protected anchorages, even within very crowded harbors. *Echo* has fixed shallow keels below each hull, giving her about 2.7-foot draft. These keels are very strong and act as bumpers when going aground. We simply don't worry about going aground any more (unless the bottom is rock or a seaway is running)—even if we do go aground, the boat sits upright, in no danger.

In fact, we think shallow draft and the ability to take the ground with impunity are the biggest advantages of a cat for coastal cruising. There is rarely a worry about finding an anchoring spot or securing our boat in a storm. Many shortcuts, friendly little marinas, and shallow spots in crowded marinas are accessible to us. Score: Cat = 10, Mono = 6.

Propulsion

Our outboard has been very nice to work on, but unfortunately I am frequently doing so. I sit outside in the cockpit, with plenty of fresh air, light, and visibility—very different from the torture chambers that pass for engine rooms on most monohulls. I've taken the motor into the shop for servicing, saving lots of money. Gasoline can often be jugged from a service station. And if all else fails, we can use our dinghy motor to get us home.

We do miss the greater safety of diesel fuel, but some cats are using the new diesel outboards. Diesels are definitely more durable, so the relative cost savings of an outboard will not last over time. Also, outboards are inefficient in offshore wave conditions, threatening to commit suicide by drowning. Most outboards offer very limited charging capability, if any. Score: Cat = 4, Mono = 7.

Seaworthiness

We have taken *Echo* offshore from Beaufort, North Carolina, to Puerto Rico, returning via Bermuda to Newport, Rhode Island. We were caught out in the worst storm of our cruising lives. It was a simple cold front coming off the Carolina coast, with predicted winds of 20 to 25 knots. However, this storm soon grew into a solid force 9. We were well across the Gulf Stream and in deep water when it hit.

Luckily, Leslie had me rig our parachute sea anchor before all hell broke loose. Soon we were surfing down big seas at 8 knots under bare poles— and then the steering cables broke! The cat turned broadside to the waves until we were able to get the parachute sea anchor set up off the stern. We tried it off the bow, but it couldn't keep us pointed into the wind in those conditions. I later learned that a much bigger chute is recommended for a cat of this size, but our small one did work well as a drogue. We sailed steadily downwind at a knot or two, with the bridle preventing most yawing. I was able to fix the cables while the parachute steered the boat.

At one point in the storm we estimated the wave heights as about 30 feet, with breaking crests. Periodically a breaker would sweep over the entire boat (our cabintop is over 9 feet above the waterline), but *Echo* would bob up through the foam like a cork. Working on deck was much easier than on a monohull in similar conditions. I could go forward on my feet when I would have been crawling on our old boat. Though we were taking breaking crests aboard, the decks were usually free of green water.

Down below was not comfortable in this storm. The noise was phenomenal, causing much anxiety. Noise is one of the worst problems on our cat in storm conditions. The light construction and the bridgedeck spanning the tossing seas all act as sounding boards. This was a great contrast to our heavy monohull, which was a relatively quiet, sheltering cocoon in a storm.

The cabin did remain dry, and somehow Leslie managed to keep hot food coming out of the galley. She had to hold the pots on the stove as they wanted to fly straight up when we dropped off a wave, but the lack of heeling and rolling allowed her to provide much-needed meals.

A cat's motion is hard to describe. It can be herky-jerky to the extreme. When we are going to weather in a chop, the boat seems to fly off the top of each wave, only to crash into the next crest. There is little heeling, but there are lots of quick accelerations in many directions. My wife finds this motion more seasick-making than the monohull's slower, steadier rhythms.

Downwind is a different story. There is hardly any rolling on a cat, and little fear of accidental gybes. We can run comfortably in conditions that would have been white-knuckle sailing in our previous boats. This is a great advantage in large offshore waves. We do find that the boat still reacts to the surface patterns of the water, so if the sea is rough the motion can be jerky.

Reaching is great fun in protected water or in moderate conditions offshore. The cat really flies, and the ride is quite comfortable. Returning from Bermuda we averaged around 8 knots for nearly 24 hours after crossing the

Gulf Stream. But when the sea kicks up, we feel it is best not to take the seas right on the beam.

We took a huge breaker on the beam while trying to make San Juan, Puerto Rico. Conditions were rough, with the wind gusting over 30, creating short, steep seas. It was in the middle of the night, and I only had time to hang on, as I saw the white foam coming at the last minute. I was under water in the cockpit, while the boat seemed to tilt up to a 45-degree angle! I believe our shallow keels let the boat slip sideways down the face of the wave, preventing a capsize. I fell on my back in the cockpit, where I could see the top of the sea reaching up to the first reef point in the mainsail—about 15 feet above sea level. I'm convinced this wave would have caused a severe knockdown in most monohulls, so we felt lucky to come through it in one piece and upright. Score: Cat = 8, Mono = 9.

Speed

How fast does *Echo* go? Twelve knots once, 5 or 6 knots frequently, and occasionally all day at 7 or 8. Disappointing? Well, yes and no. We would all like to experience those 20-knot runs so prevalent in multihull lore, but we cruisers are dragging around our homes and all that goes with them.

We do tend to average better than most monos our size, but not necessarily better than bigger cruising boats. On a recent run of 40 miles down Chesapeake Bay, we averaged over 7 knots before a 20-to-25-knot breeze.

Echo rarely fails to make offshore daily runs of over 100 miles and often turns in averages around 120 or 130—not spectacular, but reasonable for a boat less than 30 feet on the waterline. We've noticed that most cruising monos under 40 feet rarely do better.

A problem we have found is the necessity to nurse the cat along in bad conditions. You cannot hang onto sail until the last minute, so you find yourself reefing and unreefing all the time. Whenever a dark cloud threatens, down comes the main. At night we are particularly cautious and reef at dusk if we are in any doubt about the weather. This means we often do not sail at our optimum speed. Combine this with the likelihood of being overloaded, and we find small cruising cats average about the same speed as monos when traveling offshore.

When the wind falls really light, we keep ghosting along. We once managed to beat a gale into Bermuda, while other cruisers were motoring in the nearly calm conditions.

Our boat's weak point of sail is to windward. There's simply nothing like a deep-keeled heavy mono when slugging to windward for days. Racier multis can fly to windward, but I imagine the motion must be phenomenal. Our old Aage Nielsen would take us comfortably to windward in winds up to 25 knots, and she'd keep going reliably up to 40. Our cat is uncomfortable on a beat if the wind is above 15. I'm not sure if we could make progress off a lee shore in a gale—we studiously avoid those situations.

Lastly, I must admit sadly to one of the cat's great failings—it drives like a bus. I miss my heeling monos, with their rails down and the tiller connecting me to the boat like the reins of a thoroughbred horse. On the cat you simply turn the wheel to turn the boat—little feedback, no fuss, no charm. The steering works great under autopilot because of the lack of steering difficulties, but I sure miss that wonderful feel. Score: Cat = 8, Mono = 7.

Storage

Both an advantage and disadvantage of the catamaran is its tremendous interior volume. Despite a displacement of under 10,000 pounds fully loaded, our documented tonnage (based on volume) is 21. We have loads of storage space, but we really shouldn't fill it up. Excess weight affects our cat's performance dramatically, where we never noticed it on our heavy-displacement boat. Unfortunately, there is a certain minimum load that every cruising boat must have, all of it essential to a safe and happy cruise. From our experience, a 32-foot cat is about the minimum size that can carry an adequate load for extended cruising with a couple on board, and possibly two small children. As it is, we are overloaded when making offshore passages, and we have a difficult time storing adequate quantities of water, fuel, and food. I think a larger cat might win, but in small sizes the mono has the edge. Score: Cat = 6, Mono = 9.

What's the score?

Taking a simple averages of the scores, our cat comes in at 7.25, our mono at 7.37. Interesting, because I would have given the nod to my cat before I sat down to categorize my preferences. The small difference in the numbers mirrors my own feelings.

I am not a multihull proselytizer, as are so many converts. My criteria are based on my specific circumstances—a liveaboard family, the need to carry large quantities of stores over long distances, a boat that is a true home.

By Beth Leonard

SHOULD YOU GET A BIGGER BOAT?

The advantages of a 35-footer over a 25-footer and a 45-footer over a 35-footer are more space, stowage, speed, and stability. The downsides are higher expense, sailhandling loads, and a reliance on machinery and mechanical aids. So what's the right size boat for you?

Y ou love your boat. She's easy to handle, forgiving to sail, not too expensive to maintain. She's taught you and your family almost everything you know about sailing. You always look forward to your time aboard, always feel sorry when it's over. Yet lately you and your sailing partner find yourselves voicing traitorous thoughts.

"If we had just a bit more stowage space...now that the kids are bigger...another cabin for guests...just another knot of speed and we could reach...if she were just a bit more stable I'd be willing to..."

Though you may have hardly admitted it to yourself, you're starting to wonder if your boat's just a bit too small, if perhaps it's time to make the leap to a bigger boat. You won't be alone: In the last two decades, average boat size has increased quite dramatically for coastal and offshore boats.

My sailing career started in the early 1980s aboard my parents' 25-foot Bristol Corsair; they're now sailing a 32-foot Ericson, and all of their sailing friends from that period have stepped up to bigger boats. When my partner, Evans, and I circumnavigated, from 1992 to 1995, our Shannon 37, *Silk,* came in about average in size. Over the course of the last year cruising aboard our new 47-foot Van de Stadt–designed sloop, *Hawk,* we've again found our boat is of about average size in anchorages from Nova Scotia to the Caribbean. Indeed, in the 1999 ARC (Atlantic Rally for Cruisers) the boats averaged 46 feet in length.

Size certainly does have its advantages, and they're obvious to anyone who's ever spent time on a sailboat. But size has its disadvantages as well. Whether going from 25 to 35 feet or 45 to 55 feet, a bigger boat costs more—it's more expensive to buy, to dock, to cruise, to maintain. And the disadvantages don't stop there. By sharing our experiences in making the 10-foot leap from a 37-foot to a 47-foot boat, I hope to help you take a good look before you leap so you can make the right decision for your situation. Here are some things to keep in mind: The across-the-board

What do you want out of sailing? How much can you put into sailing? Smaller boats (above) are simple and easy on the budget. Mid-sized boats (right) let you cruise with family and friends. Larger boats (opposite page) offer more luxury and space—at a price

photos by Tom Linskey

escalations in the 10-foot leap from 35 to 45 feet are higher than in the leap from 25 to 35 feet, and higher still in the leap from 45 to 55 feet. Also, the types of boats that Evans and I jumped from and to, as well as our particular needs and requirements, may be different from yours.

What we expected: The good news

We expected certain benefits from our move up in boat size, and we haven't been disappointed; we have indeed gained stability, speed, and space. But our ranking of the importance of these, along with exactly how they've translated into pluses aboard *Hawk,* has in many cases surprised us. The biggest overall benefit has been a radical increase in our self-sufficiency,

something we had only implicitly considered before we moved aboard.

Space. We chose to devote most of *Hawk*'s 10 feet of extra length to watertight compartments in the bow and stern and a large sail locker forward. As a result, we don't have much more usable interior length than we did on *Silk*—but we do have much more space. *Hawk*'s 3 additional feet of beam translate into a tremendous amount of interior volume. Some of that volume has been dedicated to our rather idiosyncratic needs: an engine/ work room for Evans and a writing desk and credenza for me. The majority became stowage—twice as much water and fuel as *Silk* carried, three times as much clothing storage, twice as many large compartments dedicated to food, four times as many bookshelves, and five times as many toolboxes. This in turn translates into much greater self-sufficiency. We carry the

Bigger Boat, Bigger Budget

	(cost estimates are for new, moderately priced production boats)			
Boat length	25 ft	35 ft	45 ft	55 ft
Insured value	$54,000	$132,000	$288,000	$546,000
Monthly payment	$450 (15yr, 9.25%)	$949 (20yr, 8.9%)	$2,035 (20yr, 8.75%)	$3,880 (20yr, 8.75%)
Insurance (annual)	$404	$801	$1,445	$3,025
Berthage (season @ $110/ft)	$2,750	$3,850	$4,950	$6,050
Storage ($2.50/sq ft)	$531	$1,050	$1,575	$2,131
Maintenance and upgrades	$540	$1,320	$2,880	$5,460
ANNUAL OPERATING COST	$9,625	$18,409	$35,625	$63,230

tools, spares, and materials to fix just about anything on board. We have adequate diesel, food, and water to effectively double our cruising time away from "civilization."

Stability. A larger boat has advantages, as stability increases dramatically with boat size (for similar-type boats, stability tends to vary as length × beam^3). But smaller boats can still be perfectly safe so long as their limits are respected. In conditions where *Hawk* will happily keep sailing, we would have heaved-to on *Silk*. We might not have been making miles toward our destination, but we would have been safe. *Hawk*'s stability and her ability to sail well to windward keep us sailing in a lot of conditions where she's far happier than we are. For the conditions we've encountered so far, which include some tough windward work off Nova Scotia and a fast passage to Bermuda, increased stability, resulting in more rapid motion, corresponds more to increased seasickness than to increased safety. On the other hand, given our high-latitude sailing agenda, we might well encounter the extreme conditions in which increased stability is the difference between being upright and getting knocked down. This was a prime consideration in our decision to move up to a bigger boat.

Speed. Here again, size does matter, but perhaps not as much as theory might indicate. In the 1999 ARC boats finished an average of 5 hours earlier for each additional foot of length overall. Offshore, we've averaged 175 nautical miles per day on *Hawk* compared to 135 on *Silk*.

Yet what does that speed really buy us? On a 2,000-mile passage it means we spend 11½ days at sea instead of almost 15. Yet after the first five days, once we're acclimated, we've never cared whether passages lasted two weeks or three. We're still not fast enough to avoid low-pressure systems— boats need to sustain 200- to 300-mile days to achieve that. Our increased speed actually benefits us most where we least expected it, by increasing our range during daylight hours. We can now sail some 30 percent farther between ports during the day, which has greatly reduced the need to sail at night.

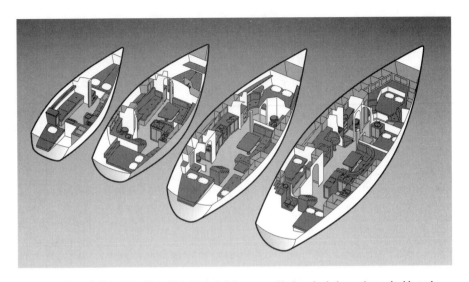

As boat size jumps from 25 to 35 to 45 to 55 feet, living space (darker shaded areas) can double and quadruple; stowage (lighter shaded areas) can multiply six- to tenfold

No matter whether you currently cruise on a lake, up and down the coast, or offshore, on a bigger boat you can expect to enjoy more space for special activities, guests, or growing children. Your cruising range will increase in terms of both the miles you can cover and the amount of water and food you can carry. Greater boat size will increase your comfort, if not your safety, in windy weather. If you sail the Chesapeake Bay, for example, greater range and self-sufficiency will allow you to reach the next scenic river or enticing anchorage on your weekend jaunts. If your summer vacations have been spent on Long Island Sound, a bigger boat could lead to your first cruise to Maine; if in San Diego, you might head for Baja. A bigger boat does offer tangible advantages—but it still may not be right for you.

What surprised us: The bad news

We knew there would be downsides to a larger boat, though for our high-latitude liveaboard agenda we didn't think they would begin to outweigh the benefits. We assumed the biggest disadvantage would be increased costs. Yet a year after we moved aboard, we're still coming to grips with all the implications of our 10-foot step up. None of what follows should have surprised us, but as with the advantages we envisioned, the reality hasn't always matched the theory.

Seamanship. Though *Hawk* is much more stable than *Silk*, and therefore much "safer" in extreme conditions, *Silk* was much more forgiving. If

Boat Size: By the Numbers

	25 ft	35 ft	45 ft	55 ft
Boat length	25 ft	35 ft	45 ft	55 ft
Beam	8.5 ft	11.5 ft	14 ft	15.5 ft
Displacement	5,400 lbs	12,000 lbs	24,000 lbs	42,000 lbs
Cost per pound	$10	$11	$12	$13
Boat price	$54,000	$132,000	$288,000	$546,000
Cabin area (square feet)	120	240	360	480
Stowage volume (cubic feet)	120	360	720	1,200
Berths (singles, doubles)	3, 1	4, 1	2, 2	2, 3
Heads, separate shower	1, 0	1, 0	2, 0	2, 1
Tankage (fuel, water)	18, 36 gal	40, 80 gal	80, 160 gal	140, 280 gal
Engine size	14 hp	30 hp	60 hp	105 hp
Battery bank(s)	200 a/h	300 a/h	450 a/h	675 a/h
Sail area (main + genoa)	330 ft^2	600 ft^2	1,000 ft^2	1,500 ft^2
Mainsail (two reefs, sail numbers)	122 ft^2 (Dacron)	240 ft^2 (Dacron)	400 ft^2 (Dacron)	600 ft^2 (Dacron)
Genoa (130%) (roller-furling	198 ft^2 (Dacron)	360 ft^2 (Dacron)	600 ft^2 (Dacron)	900 ft^2 (Dacron)
sun cover, foam luff-flattening pad)				
Sail cost (main + genoa)	$1,819	$4,972	$7,899	$11,935
Primary-winch rating	16	40	53	66

we misjudged a squall and didn't get the chute off in time, we could wrestle the sock down over it and manhandle the spinnaker to the deck. If we wrapped the jib during a gybe, we could unwrap it by hand in light air and with a winch in windy conditions. But brute force gets us nowhere aboard *Hawk*. She requires much greater forethought, because the forces she generates quickly become unmanageable and dangerous. The 750-square-foot mainsail needs to be reefed before a squall hits; the 1,500-square-foot spinnaker needs to be down before the wind freshens. If we wrap a headsail, we must look at how it's wrapped and turn the boat, using the force of the wind to free it. *Silk* offered the perfect learning environment while we made every mistake in the book; *Hawk* demands all the skills we've acquired to sail safely and efficiently.

Fitness. Before we started sailing *Hawk*, I'd been of the "bigger boat, bigger winches, no problem" school. But we quickly discovered that bigger winches won't carry a bigger, heavier sail bag to the bow; won't wrestle a larger, weightier anchor out of a locker; won't flake and tie down an oversized, ill-mannered mainsail; won't claw down and secure a furling sail if the furler breaks. Even where bigger winches do make a difference, *Hawk* still requires greater fitness than *Silk*. On *Silk* we could pull in the mainsheet by hand in a light-air gybe; on *Hawk* we have to winch in the sheet, which can take 3 to 5 minutes of solid aerobic exercise. On *Silk* we could raise the mainsail by hand, then use the winch to get it tight; on *Hawk* we can get the mainsail to the jumper stay with a two-to-one halyard, then we're back to grinding for minutes at a time. Only after we moved up to *Hawk* did I start to notice the direct correlation between the waterline length of racing boats and the size of the crews' necks and biceps—and they have *big* winches!

Reliance on mechanical aids. No matter how fit we are, we still have to rely on mechanical aids to handle the forces generated by *Hawk's* sails and anchors. Some sort of mechanical device needs to be between us and those forces at all times: a self-tailing winch, rope clutch, furler, or windlass. Mechanical advantage has its disadvantage(s): our two-to-one main halyard requires twice as many turns of the winch to raise the sail a foot, which means raising the sail takes more time. All of this equipment costs money, but more than that, it reduces our reaction time when trying to control a sail (put the mainsheet on the winch, take the pressure off the clutch, open the clutch, use the winch to control the sheet while easing the main) and decreases our independence and our options. We find ourselves constantly walking a fine line between controlling the forces on *Hawk* and becoming dependent on mechanical aids. For example, adding an in-mast or in-boom mainsail system would greatly facilitate handling our mainsail, but would leave us with few options if it broke.

Scale. On a bigger boat, everything is bigger. I'm about 5 feet, 4 inches tall, and on *Hawk* everything seems to be just one size too large for me. The last three loops of our ⅝- and ¾-inch docklines and sheets spill out of my hand. I'm too short to carry the light-air sails in their bags—I end up dragging them along the deck. I can't reach the top of our boom, so I have to throw sail ties over the sail and hope for the best. I can just barely reach the headboard of the main by climbing 5 feet up the mast. While things initially felt large on *Silk,* I was physically able to hold a coiled line in my hand, reach the top of both booms, carry a sail without dragging it. I've been surprised at how frustrating I find it to always be wishing I were two inches taller. Unlike on *Silk,* I have to depend on Evans to flake the mainsail and put on the sail cover.

This list translates into more money, more time, and more effort to sail a bigger boat than a smaller one. When I used to daysail with my parents aboard their 25-foot Bristol Corsair, we'd dump ice in the cooler, whip the sail cover off, and be sailing in less than half an hour. When we returned from sailing, we'd throw the sail cover back on, hose off the boat, toss our duffel bags in the car, and be on our way. If my parents didn't use the boat for several weekends in a row, they didn't feel guilty. But a larger boat means more effort to get off the dock, more time to tidy up, and more money to keep up. If the only time you have to sail is on weekends, your free time is precious. A bigger boat will almost guarantee that you spend less of it under sail and more of it at the dock. In our experience, the happiest crews sail the smallest, simplest boats, whether up and down the Chesapeake, around the Great Lakes, or across the Pacific.

What size boat is right for you?

The attitude today seems to be that you should buy the largest boat you can afford, especially for offshore work. But in considering the pros and cons of our 10-foot leap, we've come to four conclusions. First, it would have been a mistake to have started out on *Hawk*. Given our lack of experience sailing offshore, we needed a boat that would get us out of trouble, not one that would get us into it. Second, somewhere around 40 feet seems the optimal length for a "first" offshore boat—large enough to allow some privacy, small enough to be controlled without too much reliance on mechanical aids. Third, it's obvious when the time comes for a larger boat. In our case, the list of requirements for a comfortable home we would be willing to live on for a decade or more simply would not fit in 40 feet. Fourth, moving from a small, simple boat to a big, complex boat would have been a mistake for us. In keeping *Hawk* simpler than *Silk*, we've managed to minimize the increase in cost, time, and effort. But it takes discipline and dedication to keep a big boat simple, and most people don't choose to do it.

Even given lots of money and experience, boat size should still be limited by the fitness and strength of your regular crew working without mechanical aids. Can you drop a jib in gale conditions and gather it on deck if the furler breaks? Can you retrieve a storm anchor using the manual override on the electric windlass? Unless the answer to these questions is yes, you are decreasing your overall safety rather than increasing it by going to a larger boat.

But these criteria serve only to define the upper limit on boat size for you, not the optimum size. If you're still wondering whether you should move on up to a bigger boat, thinking through the answers to the following questions may help you come to a decision.

Crew size. Has the size and/or number of your regular crew increased? Are your children getting bigger and in need of privacy, or have you added another child to the family? Have you begun to sail regularly with guests aboard? Have you started racing and can't find room for all the bodies?

Cruising itinerary. Are you planning to greatly extend your cruising range within the next five years—from Long Island Sound to summers in Maine or from coastal sailing around Santa Barbara to a year in Mexico? Long term, do you hope to head over the horizon for an extended period of time? Are your anchorages typically deep enough that the greater draft usually associated with bigger boats will not restrict your cruising?

Liveaboard lifestyle. Have you decided you need to increase the comfort level aboard if you are to continue to enjoy sailing? Do you need a more stable platform as you get a little less nimble in order to feel comfortable moving around the boat? Is a real shower, a dedicated navigation station, or a genset and watermaker essential to your future well-being aboard?

Sailing budget. Can you afford to spend significantly more than what you are currently spending on insurance, dockage, and fuel? Do you want to tie up two to four to ten times as much capital in the investment a boat represents? Would you rather own a bigger boat than keep your current boat and charter once a year in an exotic location?

If you've answered yes to any of these questions, and especially if you've answered yes to several of them, a larger boat will likely increase your sailing pleasure. But if you're still on the fence, don't leap; test-sail or test-cruise 10-foot-bigger boats (a friend's boat or during a charter) before you leap. Only when the issues making you consider moving up become compelling are you likely to feel the increase in time, money, complexity, and effort have not reduced your sailing pleasure. You'll know when it's time.

By Robin Lutz Testa

SHIPPING AND HANDLING

When cruising overseas, sending and receiving urgently needed boat parts can be an onerous experience. Here's how to avoid lost shipments and customs nightmares

Sooner or later on every long-distance cruising boat there is something that breaks and has to be shipped home for repair or replacement. Or you may decide to upgrade your system with equipment from an overseas supplier and have it shipped to you. Some investigative work into customs requirements

Keep a record of all your shipping paperwork, and note the names of every person involved in your shipment

Elizabeth Wrightson

The Hand-Carry Option

If you (or a friend) are flying into the country and bringing items for the boat in your checked baggage or carry-on luggage, you must clear the items through customs on arrival. Many of the rules for shipment via courier apply. First obtain information regarding the customs requirements and practices of the arrival country. Most countries place limits on the value and type of goods that may be brought in by visitors or returning residents on a duty-free basis.

While in principle goods for foreign yachts in transit are not dutiable, customs officials may require documentation, such as a commercial invoice listing the value and description of the goods and bearing the statement "for foreign yacht in transit (boat name)," to waive duty fees. In countries where the customs service is corrupt, make arrangements with a reputable private customs broker to clear your goods at the airport.

High-value or easily damaged items such as electronic equipment are most securely transported as carry-on luggage. Checked baggage can be lost, damaged, pilfered, or stolen. If size or other restrictions mean that your goods must go as checked baggage, remember that airline coverage limits are surprisingly low; consider purchasing supplementary baggage insurance for equipment that you can't afford to lose.

and shipping procedures will save you time, money, and frustration.

Customs duties and clearance

When you receive goods from overseas—even items that you've returned for repair—you are importing them. Most countries charge customs duties on imports: the amount depends on the nature and value of the item. Some countries levy additional taxes based on the value of the item alone or on the value of the item plus freight and insurance. The value of services, such as repairs, may also fall into the taxable category.

Goods imported by "foreign yachts in transit" are usually exempt from customs duties and other taxes. The logic behind this is that the imported goods will be "re-exported" when the boat leaves the country. But exempt or not, your shipment will usually need to be cleared through customs. The way your shipping documents are prepared can make the difference between a speedy clearance and a protracted one.

Choosing a courier

Choose a reputable international courier service, such as DHL or Federal Express, that has an office or agent in the locale where you are. Couriers are usually faster than air parcel post, can trace your shipment if it gets lost, and can clear your goods through customs (if you choose this service, make sure the cost is included in the freight charge). In countries where the customs service is

Fax Follow-Up

When shipping a part to a supplier for repair or replacement, sending a fax follow-up helps insure that your shipment has arrived and will be returned with the proper documentation.

Date: July 6, 2001

To: Long-Distance Marine Supplies

From: Foreign Yacht in Transit (your boat name)

Fax #: (country code, city code, and number)

Re: Defective radar (model and serial number)

Dear Long-Distance Marine:

This defective radar display was returned to you today via (courier name) under air waybill #xxxxxx. Please ship the repaired or replacement display to me as follows:

Bill to: • Name
• Billing address
• Credit card type, number, and expiration date

Ship to: • Name
• Foreign Yacht in Transit (your boat name)
• Local street address (not P.O. box) suitable for delivery

Notify: Name and phone or fax number of person to be notified when shipment arrives

Shipping instructions:
• Ship via (courier name) freight prepaid
• Ensure that all documents clearly state: "For Foreign Yacht in Transit (your boat name)"
• Ensure that all documents clearly state: "Repairs/replaces defective item previously returned"
• Fax air waybill number and shipping details ASAP to my attention at the fax number above

corrupt, customs clearance by the courier can help free your shipment—and protect you from being personally involved in corrupt practices.

If your shipment is too large for a courier service to handle, select a reputable international air freight forwarder. Forwarders consolidate freight to obtain better rates; a forwarder can also arrange customs clearance for an additional fee.

Contact the courier's local office before shipping and describe the transaction that will take place. Ask if your shipment will be subject to customs duties or any other taxes or fees. Make sure you know the value of your goods, and make it clear that the transaction is for a foreign yacht in transit.

With international shipments, and particularly for high-value or time-sensitive items, it is critical to be able to trace the shipment if it is lost. Make sure you obtain information about shipping details, such as the waybill and flight numbers on both the shipping and receiving ends, to enable you to track your goods.

Shipping documents

If you plan to ship an item out for repair or replacement, ask the courier if the item must first be registered with customs or another local agency to be exempt from duties or taxes when it is shipped back to you. If the person you speak with can't answer your questions, speak to the person in charge of clearing the courier's shipments through customs—usually their customs broker or agent.

In most cases, all shipping documents and invoices should clearly state "for foreign yacht in transit (your boat name)." For items being repaired or replaced, all shipping documents and invoices should also state "replacement for defective item previously returned" or "repaired defective item previously returned." Ask the courier if it would be better to have the shipment sent to the courier's office for pickup or if you should give a local street address (not a P.O. box) for delivery. Write down the names of everyone you speak with as part of your records.

If there is no international courier service or freight forwarder where you are and you must rely on registered air parcel post or general air freight, check with customs or a customs broker or agent for instructions. The latter will charge a fee for their services.

Inform the supplier

When you have all your shipping information, contact your overseas supplier, preferably by fax, and give them instructions for handling your shipment (see sidebar). Make sure they understand the importance of preparing your shipping documents and invoice exactly as instructed. If possible, arrange with the supplier for freight charges to be prepaid and billed to your credit card. Large companies usually benefit from lower freight rates, and this can save you as much as 50 percent on shipping charges. Of course, you should get a quote first.

Instruct your supplier to fax you the air waybill number of your shipment and the shipping details (date shipped, place shipped from, flight numbers, and ETA) as soon as possible. The air waybill number will allow you to check the status of your shipment and trace it if something goes wrong. The shipping details will tell you where and when the shipment actually left and when it should arrive. If you have used a freight forwarder rather than a courier, make sure you get both the forwarder's house air waybill number (the forwarder's internal tracking number for the consolidation) and the master air waybill number (the airline's tracking number).

Tracking your shipment

Monitor your shipment's progress by contacting the courier's local agent regularly. Make sure you have your shipment's air waybill number and shipping details when you call. By discovering problems early, you can take action to get your shipment back on track sooner. If there are problems with your shipment and the courier's local representative is not responsive, have your overseas supplier contact the courier's representative in their area and request their assistance. Be persistent. Keep asking questions until you get answers that make sense—or until you have the goods in hand.

IV

SAFETY

By Tom Linskey

BLUEWATER GEAR

What are the smartest, toughest gear and systems for cruising boats? Get the word(s) on choosing and using from world-cruising crews

J ust as there is no one right way to cruise, there is no single piece of equipment or onboard system that's right for every cruising boat and every crew—but some gear is more "right" than others.

That's the message I received from the crews of nine long-distance cruis-

Cream at the end of the milk run: Cruisers gather at Robertson Island, Bay of Islands, New Zealand

Leslie and Chip Babbott, Tamarack; *Seattle, WA; 3 years, 12,000 miles*

ing boats halfway around the world in Auckland, New Zealand, when I asked them about gear. As a passagemaker of more than 15,000 miles with my wife, Harriet, I chose what I judged to be a representative sample of offshore cruising boats, from traditional to performance, 32 to 50 feet, no-frills to fully equipped. But the real find turned out to be the sailors themselves.

Among them, these nine crews have 50 years of cruising experience and over 190,000 bluewater miles. For several this was their second world cruise and second offshore boat. From New Zealand most were headed west, around the world.

In my book the crews qualified as hands-on cruising gear technicians; in addition to "field-testing" their systems under ocean-sailing conditions, they had selected, installed, maintained, modified, and, in several cases, rebuilt the equipment themselves. Naturally, they had high praise for the gear that worked—the systems that made their cruising safer, more efficient, more enjoyable—and strong opinions about the equipment that failed to perform. This bunch impressed me as thorough, thoughtful, and intelligent; most important, they told me *why* things worked or didn't. Here's their well-tested advice.

Don Norris and Lois Zerbe, Golly Gee; *Long Beach, CA; 6 years, 19,000 miles*

Anchoring gear

Because cruisers spend 90 percent of their time at anchor, often in deep spots that have iffy holding ground (in Raiatea, in the Society Islands, for example, coves run 70 to 90 feet deep and there is often no alternative but to anchor in a coral bottom), anchors and windlasses are a form of insurance. The best policy? Crews told me: "Go oversize on anchors" and "install an electric windlass."

"Back home people thought we were crazy, carrying a 60-pound CQR on a 36-foot boat, but we've experienced more bad weather at anchor than at

Victoria and Arnold Finocchio, Papillon; *Ft. Lauderdale, FL;*
5 years, 15,000 miles

sea, and that big CQR has saved us more than once," said Chip and Leslie Babbott of *Tamarack,* a Cape George 36. Although the Babbotts were the only crew who carried a storm-size primary anchor, most advised going up at least one size from manufacturers' recommendations. Reason? Holding power, and the fact that in crusty bottoms a heavier anchor will dig in where a lighter one may "skate." An all-chain bow rode is considered mandatory; the chain weight helps the anchor stay set, and chain eliminates chafe worries.

Retrieval is the other half of anchoring "insurance." Said Don Norris and Lois Zerbe of *Golly Gee,* a Peterson 44, "For boats over 35 feet, an electric windlass is not only a necessity, it's a safety item." Just about every crew told of instances where their electric windlass (every unit should have a manual backup) enabled them to get the anchor up quickly and get their boat out of danger when an anchorage became untenable. A powered windlass meant they could re-anchor as many time as it took to feel right about it— all without back-breaking labor. Message? More than a convenience, an electric windlass could save your boat.

Other anchoring tips:
• Carry a backup to your primary (bow) anchor, and make it a different type; one anchor doesn't work in all bottoms. If one type can't get a bite in the bottom, the other may.
• A stern anchor is useful in tidal or tight anchorages. A dedicated stowage, rode, and roller setup makes deployment easy and fast. Danforth- and Fortress-type anchors, with their quick "grab," work best in a variety of bottoms.
• To protect the windlass from sudden high loads in surge or storm conditions, attach a snubber (15 feet of ½-

Philip and Lydia Osgood, Aria; *Seattle, WA; 6*
years, 25,000 miles

87

Carl Frost and Diane Cordeau (not pictured), Kama Lua; Norfolk, VA; 8 years, 23,000 miles

inch three-strand nylon line, with chafing gear) to the chain with a chain hook. Secure the snubber and then release enough chain that the snubber will take the full load; the high-stretch nylon line acts as a shock absorber.

Self-steering

This "extra crewmember" is the single most vital piece of passagemaking gear. Every crew I talked to recommended carrying at least two means of self-steering: either an autopilot and a backup autopilot or a windvane and an autopilot. Why a backup autopilot? Because nothing is more exhausting or demoralizing to a shorthanded crew than an autopilot breakdown. Autopilots have had reliability problems in the past, and according to the offshore sailors who use them today, there are still too many instances of units (particularly cockpit-mounted pilots) going down because of saltwater intrusion.

Why equip your boat with both a windvane and an autopilot? Because while most windvanes steer well in steady winds, even well-designed vanes have trouble with dramatic changes in wind velocity. Autopilots will often outperform windvanes when the wind is very light or fluky and while the boat is under power.

What brands and models of self-steering stand up to offshore use? It's not that simple, I discovered; reports of success and failure went across the range. What proves more important is correct installation, sizing (don't underspec; if in doubt, go up one size), and use. "Too many people work their self-steering to death," said Arnold and Victoria Finocchio of *Papillon*, who use a Monitor windvane on their Tayana Vancouver 42. "The first step is to trim the boat so she's practically sailing herself, even if it means sacrificing some speed, and *then* click in the self-steering." Tips:

Sue and Jim Corenman, Heart of Gold; San Francisco, CA; 12 years, 40,000 miles

• An autopilot that can interface with the GPS and steer to the GPS "course over

ground" is valuable in current.
• Bring a full set of parts for the self-steering.

Sails and sail handling

Sails designed and built with top-quality
materials and hardware, asymmetrical cruising spinnakers with snuffers, headsail roller-
furling, the cutter rig: For offshore work these
four things were high on everyone's list. "I'm
glad we invested in really good sails. We've
had no problems other than adding a few
chafing patches," said Philip and Lydia
Osgood of *Aria,* a Pacific Seacraft Crealock
37. As if to reinforce the point, the day I visited the Osgoods a cruising boat was towed in;
every sail in their inventory had blown out.

*Peter Cassidy (pictured), Jeff Hazelton,
Mike Brady,* Vagabond; Marion, MA; 1
year, 16,000 miles

Nearly as prickly were some of ocean cruisers' experiences with full-batten mains. "The
full-length battens are a hassle," said Steve Salmon and Tina Olton of the
Valiant 40 *Another Horizon.* "The luff slides clatter and scar the mast, the
leech hardware catches on the topping lift, and we've broken five battens."
Also cited: difficulty when reefing (when running before a squall, the battens lie onto the shrouds, making it tough to pull the sail down) and the
racket the battens make when the boat rolls in windless conditions.

In downwind sails, cruising spinnakers are in. (A dousing sock is a must.
The sock should be long enough to furl the entire sail, and the hoop must
be large and sturdy.) Poled-out headsails are out. "Double poles are just too
much trouble," said Carl Frost, who went back to a single pole aboard
Kama Lua, his and co-skipper Diane Cordeau's Island Packet 44 from
Norfolk, Virginia. Not one sailor felt that a genoa belonged offshore; their
useful wind range is too narrow, and they're a liability in squalls.

Cutter rigs received top marks for safety and flexibility. Several crews told
me, "With the cutter rig, when it gets rough we furl the jib, and we're down
to our heavy-weather headsail without having to go forward." A staysail's
area is small, but the effect is big; it can play a key role in balancing the
helm. Vic and Lorraine Klassen sought the ultimate in squall management
when they rigged *Maggie Drum,* their Whitby 42, with a Hood Stoway mainsail and roller-furling on both the jib and the staysail (one caveat: if the staysail is furling-equipped, it should be built strong enough to serve as a storm
jib.) The final word on sail handling came from Leslie Babbott: "The easier
a furling and reefing system is to use, the more you'll use it."

Navigation

The revolution is, of course, the global positioning system (GPS), the three-letter acronym that's opened up the world's cruising grounds. But the concern among bluewater sailors now is less with the accuracy of the technology than with the assumptions made by some of its users. Although there are still some reliability hiccups (one cruiser, for example, reported that he was on his fourth hand-held GPS unit in five years—the previous three lost the ability to obtain a fix), virtually every cruising boat uses GPS. Most carry two, a built-in and a hand-held.

Offshore sailors told me that the on-demand availability of GPS fixes is producing "lazy" navigators. Why maintain a log or a dead-reckoning chart position when the next GPS readout is just one second away? Even more alarming, every cruiser talked of novices taking off without a grounding in celestial navigation—and without a sextant. Is GPS the wave of the future, or the erosion of prudent navigation?

Depending on how GPS is used, it can be both. "GPS is a great device, but it doesn't make for better navigators. Boats are still hitting reefs," said the Osgoods. Part of the problem occurs when sailors "push" GPS fixes in poor visibility or bad weather, just the time when they should be giving themselves extra searoom. Another is the discrepancy between some charts (especially those compiled from turn-of-the-century surveys) and GPS reality. *Aria's* crew reported that some Fijian reefs are over a mile from their charted positions; on *Heart of Gold,* a 50-foot Carl Schumacher–designed sloop, Jim and Sue Corenman discovered that a reef pass at Rangiroa atoll in the Tuamotus was ¼ mile off.

Clearly, cruisers still need to approach landfalls with caution—especially (as with an increasing number of budget-conscious cruisers) when the charts they are using are photocopied, or photocopied and reduced. Photocopy quality varies, and without color gradation the reefs and rocks tend to merge with the rest of the black-and-white background. The Klassens advised, "If you use photocopied charts, be very careful. We go over ours beforehand and highlight any dangers with a felt-tip pen." Tips:

• Binoculars are an underrated navigation tool. Choose top-quality 7X50 binoculars that let in maximum light during dawn and dusk conditions.

• GPS readouts are best mounted where the helmsman can read them. The most useful functions: course over ground, range, and bearing to a waypoint.

• On passages, radar is useful for collision avoidance (to save battery power, turn it on for only a few minutes every hour to make several "sweeps"), for picking up low-lying islands and atolls, and in tracking nighttime squalls (the density of rain can be a clue to a squall's intensity).

Refrigeration

Alternately revered and reviled, bugaboo and boon to the cruising man and woman, refrigeration created consensus. I got the following "do this before you leave on your cruise" advice from nearly everyone:
• Add as much insulation as possible; iceboxes adequate for temperate areas won't hold the cold in the tropics. Four inches of insulation is the minimum; 6 inches is preferred.
• With icebox size, less area equals more cold; a box one-quarter the size of a home fridge is about right.
• If you're heading to hot climates, pay special attention to ensuring your refrigeration machinery is well ventilated.
• Get in the habit of maintenance checks.

As for choosing between 12-volt refrigeration and an engine-driven system, the fleet was split. "People should ask themselves whether they're willing to be married to the boat to run an engine-driven compressor on a daily basis," said Carl Frost. "If they're considering 12-volt refrigeration, they should ask whether their energy-generating capability (solar panels, wind generator) can keep up with the system's needs. Refrigeration has to work hard in the tropics."

Brand names were considered less of a factor than proper installation, debugging the system before departure, carrying out preventive checks, and bringing plenty of spares. "I carry a complete set of spare parts. Don't leave home without them, because they're bloody expensive everywhere else in the world," said Vic Klassen.

Communication systems

The information superhighway has spread its tentacles across the water, and—brace yourself—bluewater cruisers are going online. By linking laptop computers to single-sideband (SSB) and ham radios, sailors are sending and receiving email messages to and from shore stations, other boats, and computer networks via the Internet (with ham units, business communication is illegal). Using special communications software and a terminal node controller (a modem-type interface that translates computer data into audio tones), messages can be transmitted in the form of information "packets." A shore station (for example, a ham-radio operator) can then transfer the data from radio to computer and send it on its way (as a phone call to your relatives, for example, or onto a computer net as email). It works the other way, too; working through a ham contact, folks back home can leave a "note" in the cruiser's "mailbox" (if using a ham radio, an operator must be present), and even download the boat's present position, course, and speed.

Advantages for the cruiser include low cost (that is, once you've invested in a laptop, software, and modem), the ability to get through when static precludes voice transmission, and freedom from a radio schedule. The technology is not turnkey, however; sending email over the ham bands requires both a ham license and a relationship with a shore-based ham operator with like inclination and equipment.

Other ways cruisers are staying in touch with home include AT&T's SeaCall (an electronic messaging service that uses single-sideband channels), SITOR (telex via SSB), and ham-radio phone patches.

More than ever, radio—VHF, SSB, and ham—is the heartbeat and pipeline of the cruising community. At sea it's SSB and ham check-in and weather nets, which function as a clearinghouse of official and cruisers' reports. "One problem with weatherfaxes is correctly deciphering them," pointed out the crew of *Papillon*. "On passages we get a lot of our weather information from the boats ahead of and behind us."

Should you go with an SSB or a ham radio? Most cruisers have both capabilities, whether it's two radios or a modified ham or SSB unit used to transmit on both frequencies (a ham radio can be used over SSB frequencies only for distress transmissions). Several cruisers mentioned that increasing the ground plane is the surest way to boost signal strength; on their "next" boat, they'd have copper foil or screen laminated into the hull at the construction stage.

Power generation

How do cruisers feed their amp-hungry systems? There are as many ways— high-output alternators on the main engine, solar panels, wind generators, gensets, towing generators—as there are proponents of particular components.

Jim and Sue Corenman of *Heart of Gold* typify the charging-by-main-engine crowd. With a 200-amp alternator they average about 1 to $1\frac{1}{2}$ hours of engine running time per day to maintain their gel-cell batteries. "During a passage about one-third of the amps go to the autopilot and two-thirds to refrigeration and instruments: GPS, SSB radio and a weather-collecting laptop, VHF (kept on round the clock), running lights, and radar (run several times an hour as a collision watch)."

"We're a 12-volt boat," say the Osgoods on the solar-panel-equipped *Aria*. "We have four 48-watt solar panels (two Arco, two Siemens) on a specially built stainless-steel arch above the cockpit—it's important that solar panels aren't shaded, not even by a boom shadow—and we're close to being self-sufficient. If we lose our engine, we won't lose our systems."

On *Another Horizon*, Steve Salmon and Tina Olton have both solar panels and a wind generator. "We don't use the engine to charge the batteries; it's a noisy, inefficient way to make energy. In about 6 knots of wind, our Fourwinds wind generator kicks in. We can count on roughly half the wind speed in amps (7 amps from 15 knots of wind)."

On passages aboard *Kama Lua,* Carl Frost tows a Hamilton Ferris water generator. "The drag is neglible, only ¼ knot, and we start making electricity at 4 knots of boat speed. I usually get 6 to 8 amps per hour, with a top end of 12 amps."

A diesel genset with a high-output 12-volt alternator and a refrigerator compressor, all of which "just fits" in the engine room, supplies the power on *Golly Gee.* An 1,800-watt Heart inverter is used to run a microwave, vacuum cleaner, and power tools.

The no-frills alternative

One could be forgiven for wondering if cruising boats have become too complicated, the onboard systems too complex. Is all this machinery really necessary to go cruising? Once again, there is no single approach that's right for every boat and crew. The cruising lifestyle is one of choice, of personal preferences that are reflected in the equipment we take with us.

"We're the no-frills boat," says 25-year-old Peter Cassidy, who bought the 31-year-old, 32-foot Pearson Vanguard *Vagabond* with two friends, Jeff Hazelton and Mike Brady. Ten months later, after replacing the standing rigging and making a few other upgrades, they took off. Their systems are low-budget but savvy: a VHF, a hand-held GPS, a windvane, a tiller pilot. They use hanked-on headsails, get weather reports over a shortwave receiver, do without refrigeration. Are they roughing it, or just having a trouble-free cruise? Maybe both. "We have so few things that can break that we can't fix, it's actually convenient," said Cassidy. Right now *Vagabond* is headed for Australia, the next stop on the way around the world.

As are the other cruisers I talked with, the *Vagabond* crew is living out their dream of sailing away. And therein lies the beauty of cruising and cruising equipment: It helps get us where we all want to go.

By Lin and Larry Pardey

SECRETS OF SLEEP AT SEA

Whether you're sailing overnight or on a long passage, adequate sleep means safe, enjoyable cruising. Here's how to equip your boat and keep your crew well-rested

Decisions made by a tired crew are the frequent cause of groundings, pilot errors, gear failures, or crew conflicts. In storm conditions a severely sleep-deprived crew and skipper may opt to abandon their boat for a nearby ship, a one-way (and danger-fraught) ticket out of the situa-

Leeboards or leecloths ensure safe, comfortable sleep for off-watch crew

How Much Sleep Is Enough?

How much sleep do you need? The short answer is, Just enough to leave you feeling refreshed when you wake. But the right amount of sleep varies from person to person. "Short sleepers" thrive on 6 or fewer hours of sleep at night, while "long sleepers" grumble when they don't get 9 or more hours.

Humans have a prodigious capacity to endure prolonged sleeplessness and still perform in the face of almost overpowering sleepiness. Hallucinations and illusions can occur, but they are rare before 60 hours of sleep deprivation. A sleepy sailor may be able to sail a boat, but it will take him or her a little longer to plot a course or take a navigation fix, and he'll experience increasing fatigue, frequent attention lapses, declining motivation, and problematic episodes of "micro-sleep."

Sleep researchers have shown that the brain remains quite active during sleep. It reorganizes and stores the information it receives during the course of the day and replenishes its supply of norepinephrine and serotonin, chemicals that carry electrical messages from one neuron to another. Depletion of these neurotransmitters causes the mental sluggishness that afflicts most of us late in the day.

Sleep cycles

After you fall asleep, you pass through four stages of progressively deepening sleep called non-rapid eye movement (NREM) sleep before emerging into a light sleep state called rapid eye movement (REM) sleep (so-called because the eyes dart about during this phase). REM and NREM sleep alternate in 90-minute cycles throughout the sleep period, but an increasing proportion of each cycle is taken up by REM sleep. "Delta sleep," the deepest stage of NREM sleep, and

REM sleep are the most vital phases of sleep. The greater your sleep deficit, the greater the intensity and duration of these phases in subsequent sleep periods. That's why you have such intense dreams during your first full night's sleep after a spell of prolonged sleeplessness.

The amount of sleep needed to bounce back from extreme sleep deprivation varies widely between short sleepers and long sleepers. A couple of 4-hour naps might restore a short sleeper, but a long sleeper might need 2 to 3 days of rest to catch up completely. The human body is pretty efficient catching up on sleep, passing quickly through the lighter stages of sleep to restorative REM sleep.

Sleep has a daily, or "circadian," rhythm. During daylight hours, sunlight striking the retinas inhibits the pineal gland, a pea-size structure in the brain that acts as a daily clock, from producing a hormone called melatonin. But as darkness falls, the pineal gland starts to secrete melatonin into the bloodstream. The hormone permeates every cell in the body and imposes order and rhythm on the body's myriad metabolic processes, much the way a maestro directs orchestral elements to produce a symphony. And, as the prime regulator of the sleep-wake cycle, melatonin induces sleep.

Sleep habits at sea

Standing watch day and night will disrupt your sleep-wake cycle and desynchronize your body clock, but maintaining the same watch routine will help both short sleepers and long sleepers get some hours of needed REM sleep.

Causes of insomnia to avoid include diet pills, antihistamines, certain antidepressants, asthma and thyroid medica-

96

tions, some blood-pressure medications, and cold remedies.

To stay rested over the length of a passage, try to develop these sleep habits:
- Unwind before going to bed.
- Don't go to bed until you are sleepy. If you don't fall asleep within 20 minutes, get up and read a book or practice your knots until you feel sleepy again. Get out of bed when you are done sleeping.
- Sleep in the same bunk every off-watch. The cabin should be quiet, dark, and cool.
- Don't go to bed hungry, but don't gorge before bedtime either.
- Don't drink coffee or tea within six hours of bedtime, nor alcohol within three hours of bedtime.
- Don't take prescription or over-the-counter sleeping pills (see below).
- Avoid excessive napping. One nap of about 45 minutes duration before 1500 is fine, however.
- Try to get at least 30 minutes of vigorous physical exercise every day, preferably in the afternoon or early evening. Exercise elevates your mood and helps you fall asleep faster and sleep more soundly.

Melatonin supplements

Melatonin may be your ace in the hole in fighting sleep deprivation. Many people have found that minute amounts (less than 0.1 mg) of melatonin, a synthetic supplement available in most health food stores or pharmacies, helps them to fall asleep at any time of day. Melatonin helps induce sleep in 20 to 30 minutes, and generally wears off in 3 to 4 hours. If awakened for an emergency, the sleeper will experience only a normal sleep-like grogginess—not the tough-to-fight-off, overpowering effect of a sleeping pill.

Researchers have yet to find any ill effects of melatonin supplementation. Unlike prescription and over-the-counter sleep medications, melatonin does not suppress REM sleep, cause morning grogginess, or lose its effect over time, nor is it addictive. I recommend that you keep a bottle of melatonin in your medicine chest and use it whenever you find yourself tossing and turning. For sailors, "nature's sleeping pill" may prove as restful as a warm dry bunk.

—Paul G. Gill, Jr.

tion. In contrast, people who bring their boats safely through the same storm invariably say, "We did everything we could to make sure everyone on board got some rest."

Getting rest isn't always easy, but there are important ways to improve your chances. Some start when you are planning your boat's interior, and others happen at sea. The easiest ones to implement are those affecting your onboard, at-sea scheduling.

Making rest a priority

One rule we've learned the hard way is: Start watches promptly at 2000 hours (or before dusk) even if you are on a one-day passage, even if the harbor entrance seems only a short distance away, even if you still have daylight. Time and again, tides, strong currents, adverse winds, or engine failure can delay what looks like a certain just-at-dusk port entry. Having one watch belowdeck getting some sleep is like insurance; their well-rested decisions could be the deciding factor in a difficult situation later on.

On a shorthanded cruising boat it may pay to heave-to just before making a landfall so that the whole crew gets some extra rest. Make sure you have sufficient sea room before you heave-to; a changing wind could put you ashore. If there is any doubt about your position, heave-to and wait for dawn, but continue your watches. The more comfortable motion and lack of concern about running full speed onto a reef will help you get the rest necessary for making proper decisions.

During the first few days at sea, almost everyone on a boat feels tired. The motion of the boat and the excitement of last-minute preparations and farewell parties all contribute to this weariness. Tiredness can also be a sign of seasickness and is often the only symptom displayed by those with strong stomachs. So plan on arranging extra sleep until the crew gets its sea legs.

Yet it's hard to fall asleep at 2000 in a strange bunk with the unusual motion, especially if it's still light. Try to start any voyage early in the day so the crew won't have to bunk down only a few hours after leaving the harbor. Avoid coffee, tea, or chocolate drinks for 4 hours before your watches start. Plan a daily routine that includes some quiet time as evening approaches, soothing music before dinner, and a leisurely but somewhat heavy meal within an hour of 2000 if the crew isn't prone to seasickness (seasick crew will usually fall asleep easily, and it is best to have them take the first off-watch).

If one of us aboard *Taleisin,* our 29-foot, 6-inch cutter, is unable to sleep for more than 40 minutes the first night out, we change places and restart the watches. Then a motion-sickness tablet, such as Dramamine or Stugeron, taken 30 minutes before the sleepless one's off-watch assures a good sleep—without the side effects of a sleeping pill.

Improving sleep conditions

To help the off-watch sleep, quiet down or stop every rattle possible before they get in the bunk. A can rolling around in the locker under your bunk can wake you every time you almost doze off. If the person on watch can leave the helm, it pays to take a stroll throughout the boat past sleeping crew at least every hour. This seems to subconsciously reassure sleepers that all is well. The skipper who doesn't quite trust his crew is rarely going to get enough rest; take time before any voyage to be sure each person on board knows basic sailing and emergency procedures. Let it be known that calling the skipper on deck when something is amiss is the right thing to do.

If your whole crew realizes it is easier to handle a situation before it becomes an all-hands-on-deck affair, everyone will sleep better. When we delivered a 60-

foot ketch across the Atlantic, I didn't like the look of some clouds forming astern. Although Larry had just crawled into the bunk, I called him up, and we decided to drop everything except the jib even though there was only 15 knots of wind. Twenty minutes later the clouds covered us and we roared along in a 30-knot squall, perfectly canvased. The rest of the crew never woke up.

Sleep and the watch system

We usually stick to the same watches throughout a passage. With a small crew this works well, since research has shown our bodies and minds adjust more easily to an unchanging schedule. We stand 3 hours on and 3 off, with Larry taking the first off-watch right after dinner. We stand formal night watches at all times. Three hours seems to give the sleeper enough time to really rest, yet the watchkeeper doesn't seem to get bored. When we have crew with us on deliveries, we often shorten watches to 2 hours per person so the sleeper gets 4 hours off, 2 on.

Our 3-on-3-off watch system does mean only 6 hours of formally scheduled sleep per person per night. For overnights this is usually sufficient. But on longer passages we try to take a nap at least every second day, even if it doesn't lead to a deep sleep. Mid-afternoon, a time when all chores are finished and winds are often at their steadiest, is a good time for napping.

Call the off-watch at least 5 minutes before the hour if you have a self-steering system and are sailing in relatively settled conditions. But when the off-watch must be fully alert, kitted out, and on the helm ready to go, 10 or 15 minutes warning is required. Inform waking crews immediately of any nearby shipping or shore lights so a glimpse of lights close abeam doesn't give them a start. Make sure any important navigational changes or sightings are noted on the chart or in an open logbook. Wait until the end of the switchover period, when new watchstanders will be more fully awake, to explain any course changes or details.

Equip your boat for sleep

Many boats have storage lockers in the space created by the curve of the hull next to bunks. The lockers' hard fronts make sleeping in a seaway less than comfortable. Installing shockcord-supported canvas hammock bins here instead provides both efficient, expandable storage for spare pillows and gear and excellent padding for sleeping crews' elbows and hips.

All-white or light-colored interiors make a boat's interior seem more spacious, but darker, subdued colors and nonpatterned fabrics are more restful and conducive to the feeling of security that helps promote sleep. This is especially true in the tropics, where the outside glare can be tiring and a darker interior will seem cooler and more soothing.

Provide good air circulation into the foot of each bunk for tropical conditions; an opening vent or bunk ends formed of slats with 1/2-inch gaps is better than a solid bulkhead. Even better are dorade-type ventilators that can be kept open in wet conditions. Try to get good airflow throughout the sleeping area, but avoid drafts right onto the sleeper's head.

Leecloths are softer and more comfortable to sleep against than leeboards, but make sure the leecloths' three hooks are strong enough to take twice the weight of the sleeper; also, each hook should be strong enough to support a stumbling crew who grabs the leecloth. Locating the first and third hook slightly beyond the bunk permits hanging a temporary curtain to block the light.

We've found two sleeping bags zipped together work best at sea. It is easier to get into and out of a double bag, the bag under you keeps you insulated from chilly bunk cushions, and you don't lose the blankets because of the boat's motion. We carry four bags, two summer weight (2-ounce fill) and two winter weight (4-ounce fill). We stuff the spare bags into bolster pillows made of the same soft farbic as our upholstery. This gives extra bedding for guests and extra pillows to use in the main cabin.

To keep the sleeping bags clean, we have sewn together two 50 percent cotton, 50 percent Dacron sheets to form liners. In the tropics, the liners become our sleeping bag with a light blanket available just in case. Washable Dacron-filled pillows are best for sailing. Rubber attracts moisture and smells; down-filled pillows tend to start leaking after a year onboard and can't be cleaned easily.

Sleeping is just as important to the success of a voyage as good food and compatible crew. By carefully considering your watch schedule and sleeping arrangements, you can ensure an alert, amiable crew when you need them most.

By Lin and Larry Pardey

SAFE AND SECURE

Choose a leaving place; bring your own anchors or tie to a mooring; select a marina berth, dry storage, and decommissioning—Lin and Larry discuss these issues and more

We were sitting under *Seraffyn*'s cockpit awning nibbling steamed Mexican clams, foraged that morning from a Sea of Cortez mangrove lagoon, when another boat motored around the point. "You Larry and Lin?" called its owner. "Fellow over in La Paz said you do

Taleisin *moored to her own anchors and secured on deck: mainsail cover lashed, boom tent protecting brightwork, fenders ready for the caretaker's dinghy*

Carry replacement parts and check the wear on mooring components yourself. Here, Larry replaces the suspect swivel, shackles, and pennant of a commercial mooring

delivery work. Come on over and have a chat."

Three hours later we were back aboard our 24-foot Lyle Hess–designed cutter and feeling pretty excited. If we signed on to do the delivery, we could top up our cruising kitty. Then it hit: To deliver the boat meant leaving *Seraffyn,* our most precious—and uninsured—possession, in an area that, back in 1969, had no marinas, yacht clubs, or facilities for visiting cruisers.

The night-long debate that followed set the tone for the rest of our cruising lives. Larry summed it up: "We have to decide whether we own our boat or our boat owns us."

This is a question both weekend and long-distance cruisers will face, whether they are leaving their boat to go sightseeing for an afternoon and evening or fly home suddenly in an emergency. Learning how to leave your boat behind for a weekend or several months in safe circumstances can help you feel that you own your boat, not the other way around.

Choosing a leaving place

Before you choose between a mooring, your own ground tackle, a marina berth, or long-term dry storage, you need to address several major concerns. First, no matter how attractive it may seem, don't leave your boat out of reach in a hurricane-prone harbor. Your boat can be damaged by flying debris or sunk by wind-driven tidal rises that can float marina pontoons off their pilings. If you have no other choice, assume there will be a hurricane during your absence and prepare the boat for the worst.

In areas subject to sudden, extreme winds, avoid berths with more than ¼ mile of fetch (open water). The floating dock to which we'd tied 29-foot, 6-inch *Taleisin* in Newport Harbor, California, was literally torn apart when a Santa Ana wind began gusting to 90 knots across ¾ mile of open water. Fortunately, a 65-pound Luke fisherman anchor we'd kedged out held both boat and dock.

If there are several equally well protected locales to leave your boat, choose the one that offers the most safeguards against theft. An unguarded marina lends easier access to your boat than does a mooring, where intruders are more visible. In areas with security problems, choose a locked marina with nighttime patrols.

Narrow rivers in areas prone to heavy rain can be dangerous. A few years ago over 200 boats moored in the Kerikeri River in New Zealand were damaged, lost, or driven downriver when floodwaters ripped out moorings, wharves, and pilings.

Hull material is also a factor in deciding between a mooring, a marina berth, or dry storage. We prefer leaving wooden-hulled *Taleisin* on a swing mooring. During various winds and tides she will expose different parts of her hull to the sun, reducing localized ultraviolet deterioration, shrinking, and cracking, an important consideration for any wood hull.

Your own anchors or a mooring?

You can use your boat's ground tackle to set your own mooring (see figures). Look for a spot with lots of swinging room, well away from the main channel and any racing marks. In an area known for strong winds from one direction, try to be the windward boat; if a neighbor's mooring pennant fails or his anchor drags, you won't be in the path. For short forays we usually set a second anchor on its own rode and ask someone on a nearby boat to check our boat.

We never leave our boat moored or anchored in an open roadstead (an exposed shore) overnight. Even in trade-wind areas abnormal onshore winds can develop, turning the anchorage into a dangerous lee shore. Any anchorage that doesn't offer the 360-degree protection of a landmass should be viewed with suspicion.

Don't use a mooring without inspecting it first. We've risked insulting mooring owners in many parts of the world by lying to our own anchor until we could dive and check the mooring. The results of these inspections have reinforced our resolve; three out of five had defective or badly worn components, most commonly undersized or worn shackle pins. We carry a stock of ⅝-inch galvanized shackles for such occasions.

Moorings can offer some safety advantages. Should another vessel collide with your moored boat, your boat can shift away to minimize damage. With one or two mooring pennants covered with plastic hose and led through bow rollers onto winch drums (or to bitts designed to take anchor strains), there is little risk of chafe or stress to gear.

It is also easier for a hired caretaker to inspect a mooring line for potential problems. In a marina, the same caretaker would be tempted to take a

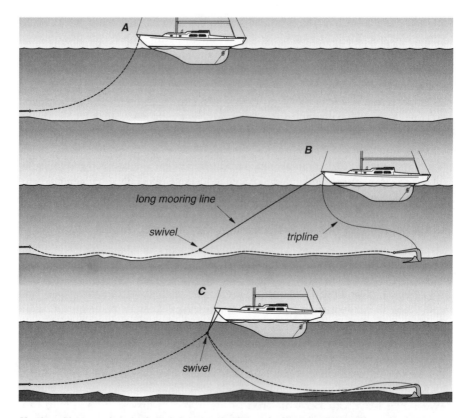

Mooring with two anchors (and all-chain rode). (A) After anchoring normally, shackle a swivel with a long mooring line to the middle of the anchor chain. (B) Reverse slowly with engine, or drift back with wind or current, paying out mooring line and remainder of chain. Attach a second anchor to end of chain and lower with a tripline. (C) Pay out the tripline and winch the mooring-line swivel up from seabed (this will help set the second anchor). (D) (opposite page) Secure the end of the tripline below the swivel. Add a second mooring line to the swivel and lower it to below the depth of the keel. When mooring with three anchors (opposite page, bottom), secure the third anchor's nylon rode to the chain just below the swivel

quick look and move on. Access to a moored boat is harder for thieves (but in areas frequented by small fishing boats the opposite can be true, especially when a moored boat looks deserted).

Selecting a marina berth

A guarded marina berth is the best choice in high-theft areas or when cost, sun, and heat damage are not overriding factors. If possible, locate your boat away from vessels with arrays of electronic gear or permanently rigged

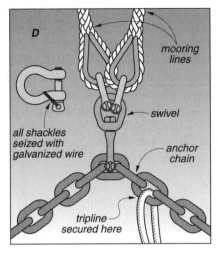

D

mooring lines

swivel

all shackles seized with galvanized wire

anchor chain

tripline secured here

shore-power cables, which increase the chance of electrolysis. To reduce the odds of collision, choose a berth removed from bareboat charter fleets, sailing schools, and training vessels.

Situate your boat in the vicinity of liveaboard boats; marina operators report that liveaboards reduce theft and other hazards. After we left *Taleisin* moored in a harbor in Fremantle, Western Australia, and moved ashore, a 45-foot racing boat docked in the marina exploded into flame at 0100. Half a dozen liveaboard sailors pushed the blazing vessel out of its berth and clear of other boats, and secured so it could not drift down onto *Taleisin*.

As a chafe guard, slip unsplit nylon-reinforced PVC hose over each dock line; then, to make sure people in adjacent berths don't uncleat your lines, run it through the base of the cleat on the dock and tie it with a tight bowline. Then adjust it on the deck of your boat. The only way someone can untie your boat is to board it.

Before you leave your boat, study the mooring-line arrangements used by well-maintained local boats. If they have specialized snubbing gear such as chains and weights, rubber bungies, or doubled-up lines, invest in similar gear. A marina that is wonderfully calm during one weather pattern can be subject to prolonged heavy surge in another.

Dry storage

For fiberglass or metal-hulled boats, hardstand storage can be the most economical way to leave your boat for longer periods. Steel or alloy boats will be less prone to corrosion and electrolysis when they are out

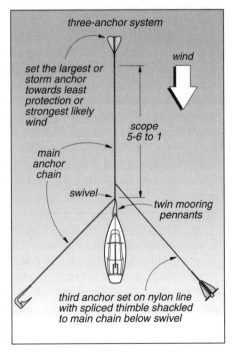

three-anchor system

wind

set the largest or storm anchor towards least protection or strongest likely wind

scope 5-6 to 1

main anchor chain

swivel

twin mooring pennants

third anchor set on nylon line with spliced thimble shackled to main chain below swivel

of salt water. Fiberglass hulls can have a dryout period to reduce or prevent moisture absorption. The cost of lifting the boat out of the water can be justified by taking the opportunity to paint the bottom on your return.

Before you book your haulout, check the worst-case figures for high tides and storms in the area. If the storage yard is located in a large bay and is situated only a few feet above high water, it could be awash in a storm. When there is a choice between storage yards, choose the one on higher ground.

Ask the yard manager to place your boat out of the path of Travelifts and boat-moving machinery. Your boat should be positioned bow-to the strongest expected winds and preferably next to boats with low centers of gravity, such as powerboats and multihulls. Finally, no matter how secure the cradle looks, no matter what assurances the yard personnel give you, inspect the cradle yourself. You might find a cracked weld or a worn, corroded bolt that a less conscientious person would miss.

Caretakers and decommissioning

To make leaving our boat safer, we hire "active insurance," a caretaker who will inspect the mooring lines, wash down the boat twice a week and open it up once a week for airing, and check the bilges. We try to choose a person who is capable of taking action if problems occur. In South Africa, for example, our caretaker was a professional diver and boatbuilder who lived aboard his workboat 300 yards from *Taleisin*. It pays to make the caretaker relationship a professional one; accepting the free offer of a newly met friend or a cruising buddy is a risky way to save money. If things start going wrong, your friend may not be able to look after your boat.

In theft-prone areas we pay someone to sleep aboard. In Mexico the 16-year-old son of a Canadian cruising family was delighted to earn $5 a night this way; he also helped by warning off skippers who would have anchored too close and fouled *Taleisin's* ground tackle. If your boat is moored in a nondemarcated mooring zone, instruct the caretaker to light an anchor light nightly. This keeps the boat from appearing deserted and helps to protect you legally in the event of a collision.

Don't discuss your departure over the radio. We listened while cruisers in Mexico chatted about their holiday plans. Later, workmen at a local shipyard told us about translating this broadcast.

In poorer countries, where one piece of boat gear could cost as much as a person's yearly salary, remove visible signs of electronic gear, such as aerials, that will tip off thieves. Consider finding someone who is willing to lock up your equipment (especially easily fenced electronic instruments, inflatable dinghies, and outboard engines) in a garage or basement on shore. Then remove deck hardware, solar panels, deck-stored sails and roller-furling sails, as well as canvas work such as dodgers and seat covers. This will cut down on sun damage and present less windage during storms.

Tie extra lines around your mainsail cover to prevent flogging and chafing. Consider lashing a heavy-duty canvas cover over the boom and out to the toerails to protect varnish or paintwork on the deckhouse. Synthetic carpet, fuzzy-side down, makes a perfect protector for brightwork. Lash it securely with nylon twine.

If you are leaving your boat in foreign storage, the final step is to check the legalities with customs and immigration officials. For example, in South Africa we needed a reentry visa added to our passports explaining that we were returning to a boat in temporary storage. Without that visa we would have had to post a repatriation bond of $3,000 to return to *Taleisin* after our four-wheel-drive African safari.

Twenty-six years ago we learned how to leave *Seraffyn,* and we've used that knowledge many times since, reassured by the fact that we've invested our money and time into preventing problems. The ability to leave our boat in worry-free safety has added tremendously to the personal freedom we've discovered in cruising.

CREW CARE

V

By Diana Jessie

CHOOSING A CRUISING CREW

"We don't take guests," says bluewater cruiser Diana Jessie. For passagemaking, compatibility is the key issue in choosing crew. For coastal cruising and club racing, it's compatibility plus–an exercise in filling in the skills and experience you need on board

I n the 14 years my husband, Jim, and I have sailed *Nalu IV*, our Lapworth-designed 48-footer, we've had more than 100 different people aboard as crew. Easily 80 percent of them are on our repeat list. Some are family and some old friends, but at least half were total strangers

Pitching in: One of the most desirable crew attributes is noting tasks and doing them

111

when we picked them up in ports around the world.

Both insurance requirements and good sense dictate taking extra crew on long passages. Jim and I have sailed about 10,000 miles alone, but *Nalu IV*, which has neither self-steering gear nor roller-furling, requires crew to steer and handle her sails. We also think it is important that two people be on deck at night. Besides, we enjoy the company and camaraderie of sailing with crew.

There are endless tales about bad experiences with crew. We've made some mistakes, but in time we've learned to make good choices. We've learned, too, that our parameters for selecting and living with crew work just as well with family and old friends as they do with strangers. In fact, we think of everyone sailing on the boat as crew; we don't take guests.

The characteristics of good crew

Finding crew candidates is not a problem. Friends write to ask for a spot on the boat; strangers seek us out in port. If we're short of candidates, we post notices in local yacht clubs or youth hostels. Compatibility, attitude, skills, personal habits, physical condition, and money are the factors we consider in choosing crew. We take the time to interview potential crew carefully, so we're as sure as we can be about our choice.

Compatibility. Compatibility is the most critical issue. We don't define compatibility as similarity, but as the ability to fit with us and each other, like pieces in a puzzle.

At first we assumed that family and longtime friends would make good crew because they would be compatible. But we found that knowing people on shore is very different from being with them in the confined spaces of a boat. On a boat there is no place to hide, to have an angry outburst, or to demand special attention. Compatibility on our part means being aware of and sensitive to the crew's needs. We are flexible about people and their duties and work at finding the right niche for each crewmember.

Attitude. Attitude is important for us. We want crew who don't wait to be told, but who step up and help with whatever chore is at hand. A self-starter is always welcome.

Skills and experience. Unlike many other big-boat owners, we find that dinghy sailors make good crew because they have learned the basics of sailing. Especially because our boat doesn't have self-steering, we value their sailing skills and find they can quickly learn other big-boat basics—steering by a compass, anchoring, and the like.

Personal habits. Personal quirks, such as sloppy housekeeping or careless personal hygiene, can't be hidden on a boat. We make our judgments based in part on the potential crew's appearance during our interview.

When Crew Becomes a Liability

When the insurance company stipulates that there must be three adults aboard for offshore passages, many cruisers choose to go uninsured. We feel that insurance is essential to protect our investment, so our choice is to take on crew.

Insurance regulations make the situation a double-edged sword. If you pay crew to sail with you, they are covered by the Jones Act, and you are required to pay heavy workman's compensation benefits. The insurance runs about $300 per month per crew, over and above salary.

If the crew pays you, your boat is considered a charter vessel. Again, your insurance rates are affected, and your status in foreign countries may also be affected. As a yacht for hire, you are expected to meet legal requirements that are not imposed on private boats.

Our present solution is to keep a file of requests to sail with us, including a note that the crew has volunteered to participate in the cost. We don't know if this situation will hold up in court as it has never been tested.

Health. Good physical condition is a crucial concern, though we do consider chronic conditions on an individual basis. We decided to take on a young man who had epilepsy after we'd learned something of his medical history. I told him my requirement was that he wear a safety harness at all times as I was not strong enough to get him on the boat if he fell off. He's sailed thousands of miles with us without any problems.

Money. We ask crewmembers to contribute a specified amount per day toward their expenses; this way they know ahead of time how much money they'll need while they're on the boat, and we have some of our costs defrayed. We don't expect the contribution (in 1995 it was $10 per day) to cover all our costs; nor do we want to take on freeloaders.

Interviewing

To keep the discussion businesslike, we conduct the initial interview in *Nalu IV*'s cockpit. Only if we are seriously interested do we invite potential crew to the belowdeck living area.

Among the questions we ask are four that help us determine if there's a good "fit": What do you expect to get from this cruise? What should we expect from you? What makes you easy to get along with, and what makes you hard to get along with?

In addition to the interview, we ask candidates to fill out a questionnaire that covers health and emergency information. It gives us a means of contacting family, if necessary; it documents health problems, chronic ailments, and allergies; it lets me know birth dates so I can surprise the crew with a birthday party. The last question on the form is, "Can you swim? How far?"

Choosing Coastal Crew: Never Assume

Crew needed: Must be experienced sailor, gourmet cook, diesel mechanic, brilliant conversationalist (who enjoys silence sometimes), and a self-starter. Your ideal might be different, but how do you find your ideal? Asking potential crewmembers for a sailing résumé and references may seem like overkill if they belong to your yacht club or sailing club, but whether you do so formally or on the sly, you must determine the skills, abilities, experience level, and compatibility of anyone you are considering as crew. The level of inquiry will depend on whether you are planning a coastal passage or a club race.

References don't have to be formal. Since the sailing community is fairly close-knit, ask fellow sailors in your marina or club what they know about a potential crewmember. Is he or she congenial, trustworthy—or whatever other qualities you are looking for? Ask whether they have sailed with your potential crew. I once chose a crewmember without asking around, and when I mentioned that he would be joining us in an upcoming race, several people volunteered that he was unlikely to be reliable in a crisis—and it turned out that he was.

Look for complementary skills. If you're a fine navigator but no good as a diesel mechanic, try to find someone with mechanical skills. Evaluate the strengths and weaknesses of the entire crew, inventory which skills are needed for the passage or race you're planning, and fill the positions accordingly. It helps morale among the crew if each crewmember feels he or she can make a unique contribution.

Try to make sure your crew is compatible. Bringing people together in close quarters with little or no privacy, highly reliant on themselves and each other,

sounds somewhat like an encounter group—and it can quickly turn into one if the crew is incompatible. Establish expectations and guidelines for drinking, smoking, and even eating. A crewmember who eats all the cookies on the first day may become an outcast even though his sail-trimming skills are excellent. Does everyone except the skipper hate country music, and what if that is the only music aboard? People don't volunteer information on seasickness proclivity or snoring or sloppy housekeeping, so unless you ask or otherwise find out, you may be in for an unpleasant surprise. If the skipper is not particularly experienced or strong-willed, he or she had better put together a very compatible crew.

Look for crewmembers with similar comfort levels for risk-taking. At the first sign of a tropical depression during a recent offshore passage, the variety of responses among my crewmembers was enlightening. One wanted to check out the storm trysail; one wanted to turn back immediately; one wanted more weather information. All could have been justifiable responses to the situation, but each crewmember's inclination to adventurousness and risk-taking and required level of comfort and safety were different. Before you go, gauge the crew's risk-taking compatibility by discussing the possibility of (and likely reaction to) bad weather or a serious breakdown.

Try to find crew who are self-starters. Unless you want to micromanage the entire passage, you need a crew with ability *and* initiative. Initiative shows itself in various ways. While daysailing with a new crewmember in preparation for an offshore passage, I noticed that this person put in a long trick at the helm without complaining and was the first to coil the sheets, bag the trash, and clean up the boat when we returned. Sure enough, during the offshore trip she initiated tasks more frequently than anyone else. I avoid crew who will do only what I ask; on an offshore passage, I don't want to keep reminding crew of their jobs.

When evaluating crew, pay attention to nonverbal signals. A crew may be telling you what you want to hear, but there will be clues that you can decipher before it is too late. Does a crewmember talk an adventurous game but appear uncomfortable when the boat heels? Perhaps he or she lacks experience or self-confidence. A crew who shows signs of fear when the bay becomes rough can be a problem when crossing an ocean. Read between the lines, understand the motives behind the answers to your questions, and above all listen with your heart.

Crew often lack control over the skipper's choice of other crewmembers and must suffer the consequences of the skipper's lack of judgment in this and other areas. So choose your crew carefully; the choices affect the safety, well-being, and happiness of everyone aboard. One last point: The compatibility issue extends to the skipper—perhaps even more than to the crew.

—Ronald L. Scott

The best answer: "Yes. It depends on what's chasing me." Most important, we've found that the form can prompt a discussion of personal issues that might not come up otherwise.

We also make sure that crewmembers have proper legal documents, especially since our legal responsibility for them is often implied if not stated outright. Until we've cleared into a new port, the skipper keeps everyone's passports; when crew leaves the boat, we note departure, flights, and other details in our log.

Speaking of legalities, some countries—French Polynesia is one—require posting a bond for each crewmember when you arrive; this is each individual's responsibility. One of our crew, who had assured us he had the money for his bond, disappeared on arrival. Fortunately, an immigration official told us that he could go nowhere without a bond and our permission to leave the boat, and we were not held responsible.

We've never used a written contract. Instead, we agree to a one- or two-day trial sail. If either we or the crew are unhappy, we go our separate ways. I'm pleased to say this happened only once.

What the crew needs to know

During the interview process, the crew find out as much about us and our boat as we find out about them. We find that it's important to make a clear statement at the outset about our boat and our program. We say up front that our boat is neither a democracy nor a commune. We own it, we're responsible for it, and we make the decisions.

We tell the crew what our destinations are and when we expect (approximately) to arrive. When we arrive at a destination, we do shore trips and our crew does shore trips. For long forays, we trade off (if needed) going ashore so someone is always on board and minding the cat.

Everyone is expected to steer and navigate, and everyone stands an equal number of watches. As owners, we stand separate watches so that one of us is always on deck to make emergency decisions.

On *Nalu IV,* each person is responsible for his or her personal space and belongings. The main saloon is shared by everyone, so we don't allow personal items to be left there. How the crew quarters are kept up is up to the crew.

When friends or family are flying in to meet us, we don't make a specific date. Instead, we suggest a time range (a date, give or take five days) and an approximate location, within 100 miles, for our rendezvous. We let them know where to check for messages if we aren't on hand when they arrive. We also let them know what to expect; a daily cost; transportation for mail and boat spares; limited communication with home.

The rewards

Our expectations may have kept some people from joining us on *Nalu IV,* but our care in choosing crew has resulted in a large number of lasting relationships. It's gratifying to us that past crew want to sail with us again. These young men and women have made it possible for us to see the world from the deck of our own boat; more important, they've given us a new view of that world.

By Laura Hacker-Durbin

GUESTS ON BOARD

Inviting family or friends to join you on your cruise can mean good times or a grueling experience. Here's how to make sure your visitors (and you) enjoy the getaway time together aboard your boat

A warm breeze astern, clear azure skies, fiery sunsets, moonlit anchorages—cruising is a fabulous lifestyle, and one that is meant to be shared in the good company of family and friends. However, as my husband, Randy, and I have found from having visitors aboard our

Here they come! Before your guests arrive, be sure to prep your boat and yourself

Tom Linskey

117

Tom Linskey

Little things: Color-coded washcloths (and towels) mean reusability by each crew, less ship's laundry for you

40-foot cat-ketch, *Pollen Path,* there is much more involved in having guests on board your boat than issuing an invitation. There are many factors you need to consider: the logistics of meeting your guests; privacy and costs (both theirs and yours); and your and their itinerary and expectations. When inviting guests on board, it's also important to realize that, as host, it is your responsibility to organize your guests' time on your boat.

Expectations and reality

The length of your guests' visit should be determined by you (not them) and dictated by your schedule. Perhaps you'll spend a weekend cruising local waters, or, as with many long-distance cruisers, the visit will run a week or more. Whatever time period you choose, be sure to plan the entire stay. They may prefer to spend part of their visit in a hotel; if so, suggest hotels that are reasonably accessible to an acceptable anchorage. If your guests are keen to go diving or snorkeling, find the best areas for this and plan your cruise accordingly. Because your guests will be using their vacation time and money to visit you, planning a holiday that accommodates their preferences helps make sure everyone will have a good time. After discussing their expectations and wishes, come up with an itinerary.

Your friends and family may believe that visiting you on your boat means sipping rum punches all day or lounging on the beach. Once they come cruising, this notion will be dispelled by necessary boat chores and, in many cases, a lack of space, privacy, or creature comforts (rum punches do figure in around sundown, though). While you're still in the discussion stage—and whether they are seasoned or novice sailors—go over issues that may cause problems, such as expenses, privacy, sleeping quarters, the use of fresh water, climate considerations (sunburn or excessive heat or cold), and seasickness, with your guests. Realize that while you are accustomed to the cruising lifestyle and local weather conditions, your visitors are not; what may be commonplace to you may be uncomfortable or seem like hardship to them. Discussing these issues ahead of time helps prepare your visitors for the realities of cruising and living aboard and helps avoid surprises.

The rendezvous

The more planning and organization of the rendezvous you do with your guests, the better. A definite, realistic arrival date lets you avoid rushing or sailing in adverse weather to meet them. At the same time, make a contigency plan—a fax depot, mail drop, radio sked, or other contact in case plans change on either end. Arrive at the rendezvous ahead of time to ready your boat for your guests' arrival: stow extra gear and empty lockers and drawers for their use; either finish major maintenance projects or put them on hold. Make sure your boat is clean and stocked with water and fuel, the appropriate charts and nav aids are aboard, and that you're ready to depart after a final provisioning. Use this pre-guest preparation time to scout the local area for museums, exhibits, restaurants, activities, tours, or other things of interest.

What to bring

Whether or not your guests are sailors, it is best to advise them about what to bring. Determine how much space in terms of lockers, drawers, or shelves you can allot to their stowage needs and ask them to pack accordingly. The climate of your cruising area will dictate what visitors should bring, but provide specific guidelines, too (for example, for cruising trade-wind areas, two bathing suits, four T-shirts, three pairs of shorts, a light-weight sweater, one dressy outfit). Advise guests about what to wear ashore; skirts or dresses are cooler and more comfortable in the tropics, for instance, and in many cases, more culturally appropriate than shorts or bathing suits. If you plan to dine out regularly, tell them to bring more than one dressy outfit.

If you have extra sets of foul-weather gear on board, your friends needn't bring their own; if you don't, suggest they bring at least a waterproof jacket. Guests should bring their own sunblock, seasickness remedy, and toiletries or medication. Make sure your boat has enough towels, sheets, blankets, or sleeping bags for visitors (ask them to bring their own to fill in any gaps). Don't forget special-purpose clothing either. For example, Randy and I like to take long walks ashore; sturdy walking shoes or hiking boots are a must.

As well as telling your guests what to bring, be sure to tell them what not to bring. Explain what footwear they'll need, such as deck shoes, reef walkers, sea boots, or dressy shoes, and that soft, duffel-type bags are more easily handled and stowed than rigid suitcases. Be patient and thorough with your explanations—often people are unaware of the limited space aboard a boat.

Guests can often bring spares or supplies for your boat (this is especially helpful if you're cruising in remote areas). We arrange for replacement gear to be shipped directly to our guests-to-be, thus avoiding extra legwork or missed connections for them. Last year, friends who visited us in Fiji brought a new masthead light, pretzel crackers, a years' worth of magazines—plus our mail. It's wonderful when guests bring Christmas with them! (Try not to go overboard with your list, however; remember that your friends and family are guests, not pack mules.)

Sleeping arrangements

The interior layout of the boat determines where your guests will sleep and the degree of privacy on board. If there is an extra cabin, they can have their own space and privacy, but if the spare cabin is chock full of gear, you may choose to give your cabin or berth to your visitors. In this case, you can sleep on the settees, in the cockpit, or tucked in amongst the gear in the "extra" cabin. Generally, we've found that hosts are more comfortable giving up their bunk than asking their guests to sleep in the main saloon. Some guests may prefer to sleep in the cockpit; be sure there's a contigency plan, such as an empty bunk, in case of inclement weather.

Food, drink, and money

Good food shared with good company is an integral part of an enjoyable cruise. Because a big part of every day is spent planning, preparing, and eating meals, before your guests arrive discuss costs, cooking, and galley duties with them. How will cooking duties be shared? Who does the washing up? How will food costs be divided? Open discussion of these subjects—tell guests honestly what arrangements you prefer—helps avoid misunderstandings.

A major food-related issue is costs. Extra people can quickly deplete your supplies. The following plan has worked well for Randy and me: Once the division of cooking duties has been decided, we make a general meal plan and a shopping list based on it (be sure to include snacks and cocktail food). We do not ask our guests to share the costs of such staples as spices, flour, rice, and oil, but they do need to contribute to the cost of provisions. We've handled the division of costs two ways, either by having hosts and guests buy the ingredients for the meals each will prepare or by splitting the total costs. You may have a different attitude and budget, so do what works well for you. Include your guests on the provisioning expedition; the wonderland of a fresh-produce market is a great way to experience some local color—and inspire the cooks.

Randy and I like to divide cooking jobs among the crew, either as individuals or as couples. We've found we have more interesting meals when we cook in turns. Sometimes we rotate duties by the meal, but more often one person or couple is responsible for meals on a given day. Decide if the cooks will do their own cleanup or if others will pitch in. Again, set up your schedule ahead of time to avoid problems later in the cruise. Since your guests don't know where everything is stowed, give them a tour of the galley, help them organize their ingredients—and then leave them to it.

Of course, things in the galley may not go the way you've planned and hoped. For example, one couple who joined us on *Pollen Path* for two weeks never felt "in the mood" to prepare any meals—despite our active encouragement. Although they did the washing up, we would have preferred that they share in the cooking duties. We didn't make a fuss, but we felt resentful about having to do all the cooking. This situation would have been avoided had we been more definite in terms of cooking arrangements.

In the pre-arrival planning phase, discuss eating at restaurants with your guests. Your cruising budget will determine how often you can eat out. If costs are not a big issue, perhaps dining ashore several times will be a part of your plan. It's best to be clear at the outset about who pays and thus avoid awkward moments when the bill arrives. In our experience, it is a treat to eat ashore with guests at least once during their stay. This gives everyone a respite from the galley, or, if you save the occasion for the last day, ends the visit on a festive note.

Drinking is another guests-onboard issue that you need to discuss. You should have (or need to come up with) a policy on when drinking is or is not appropriate. Explain your boat's rules—for example, beer is acceptable while sailing but liquor is not—immediately. Keep in mind that sailing and drinking are not necessarily a good combination, especially when the boat is your home under sail. On board *Pollen Path* we don't drink at all when under way; there are too many mistakes to be made. Instead, we enjoy wine or a mixed drink at sunset or during lunch at anchor. Ask your visitors to share alcohol costs as well.

Boat chores

Your boat is your home (or, if you don't live aboard, your second home). Some chores need to be done daily, others weekly or monthly. Do your expect your guests to help? Be fair in your requests; your time together is their weekend or vacation time. We ask guests to help with dishes, to keep their area of the boat tidy, and to do their own laundry. We take care of routine cleaning and maintenance. We do, however, make our guests feel as much a part of our daily chores as they are comfortable with.

Try to accomplish all your major onboard projects or jobs before your visitors arrive; they haven't come aboard to watch you varnish the brightwork or repair the outboard engine. If a major problem with the boat does crop up during the cruise, deal with it as best you can (this might be a good time for your guests to venture off on their own for a day). Even the closest of friends may want a break from each others' company; offer your friends the use of the dinghy for a snorkeling trip, an afternoon on the beach, or simply time alone. The best kinds of visitors are those who do not need to be constantly entertained—you might all enjoy lazy days reading novels or playing cards. Some of our guests on *Pollen Path* have been keen to participate in Randy's and my daily routine on a cruising boat, from daily radio skeds to meeting and sharing stories with other cruisers.

When you invite guests on board your boat, thorough preparation, a discussion of your boat's rules, and clear expectations will help improve the quality of your time together. At first there will likely need to be an acclimatization period for both you and your visitors, and some small adjustments may be necessary as the cruise progresses. However, once the provisioning is done, everything is stowed, and you've shoved off and set the sails, you should be set to have a great time. Cruising under sail is a magical, mystical experience—share it with your guests to the fullest.

By Laura Hacker-Durbin

TAMING THE LAUNDRY MONSTER

Clean cruisers are happy cruisers. Here's how to make the most of your boat's clothes-washing and -drying capabilities while cruising

O n board *Pollen Path,* Randy's and my 40-foot cat-ketch, the sack of dirty laundry can seem bottomless, particularly after a passage. The ease or angst of doing laundry depends on two major factors: the location and availability of fresh water and the onboard or shoreside laun-

Tom Linskey

dry facilities. Unless you have a watermaker and a washer/dryer, your laundry options are hand-washing on board, self-service Laundromats or laundry services ashore, or the "village laundry"—a source of fresh water that visiting cruisers can share with locals.

When it is possible to obtain water easily, we jerry-jug it to the boat and do the washing by hand. If water is readily available we often go on a laundry binge and wash everything—blankets, pillows, foul-weather gear—while we have the chance. In places where it is not possible to take on water, we've sent the laundry out with great results. Here are some laundry-taming suggestions from our nine years of cruising the South Pacific.

Laundry tools

If water is available free ashore, doing your own laundry is the most cost-effective method. If you have to pay for water, you need to decide whether it will cost more to buy the water or to send the washing out (hand-washing uses quite a bit of water—three 6-gallon jerry jugs to do an average load). For hand-washing you'll need several large buckets and basins, a good scrubbing brush, cold-water laundry soap, bleach, rubber gloves, and a small plunger for agitating the clothes.

Wash cycle

The most effective washing method is to soak, rinse, soak, and rinse again. Fill the buckets with soapy water and place the washing in them to soak in the sun for a few hours, agitating several times with the plunger during the "wash cycle." Scrub stains if needed. Rinse, soak for an hour or two, then do a final rinse (be sure to rinse out all the soap or clothing will be sticky when dry). Be frugal with soap—it takes a lot of rinsing to get all the suds out. Don't wash with saltwater—it takes too much freshwater rinsing to get all the salt out (laundry done this way inevitably turns damp, even if put away dry).

Dry cycle

To dry the washing, use every available inch of your boat's rigging and lifelines, and string clotheslines wherever possible (every cruising boat resembles a Chinese laundry at some point). To prolong the life of your clothing, dry it inside out, and take items in as soon as they're dry to minimize sun damage. The number of clothespins required is dictated by the wind strength: Force 1 means one or two per item; force 5 requires four clothespins or more. If it is breezy, maintain a "laundry watch" to make sure nothing disappears—this is especially important with sheets, towels, and other large items.

Laundromats and laundry services

Heaven are the places, such as marinas, that offer washing machines and dryers at reasonable rates. Before using them, ask other cruisers about the quality of the machines; some older washing machines may mangle clothing (or, as at one port in Fiji, need to be filled with a garden hose). Also determine if it is less expensive in time, money, and effort to send the washing out than to use the machines.

We have found that even the smallest towns have laundry services that are surprisingly cheap and of excellent quality. Make an inventory of what you send out to make sure it all comes back. In the South Pacific the cost of washing, drying, and folding a large sailbag of laundry ranged from $5 to $12—well worth the expense.

Nature's laundry

A river or waterfall near an anchorage offers an unlimited source of fresh water. If there is a nearby village, always ask permission to use the water, observe the spots that are used by the locals, and refrain from using products that may contaminate the water. Scrubbing on the rocks is a time-honored and effective method of doing laundry—not to mention a lovely time spent visiting with the local ladies. Waterfalls can be used as showers; observe the behavior of locals, and ask permission first. One waterfall in Fiji was fantastic; we scrubbed our clothes on the rocks, rinsed them under running streams, then plunged in ourselves for a freshwater shower.

By Lin and Larry Pardey

KEEPING CLEAN ON BOARD

Showering and bathing on board can be cramped, wasteful, and downright precarious.
Lin and Larry Pardey offer numerous solutions on keeping sparkly clean without wasting
precious water.

Mid-ocean: Trade-wind clouds, running sails pulling hard, soap and towel at the ready, the setting sun modestly silhouetting a nude sailor under a cascade of sea water from a bucket. This idyllic snapshot belies one of the realities faced by cruising sailors who venture from balmy trade-

Laura Hacker-Durbin

Sitz-Bath Solution

One way to enjoy excellent shower facilities near the companionway of a smaller boat, thus saving vital space in the middle of the cabin, is to use a sit-down sitz bath. A seated person requires 2 feet less headroom than a standing one, a tub that reaches to mid-chest height contains overspray so that a shower curtain or door is unnecessary, and an amazingly small amount of tub space allows the showerer free movement. The wooden tub we have used for years on our 29-foot, 6-inch cutter, *Taleisin*, is 30 inches wide, 28 inches deep, and 29 inches long.

Though we have never filled our tub to have a bath, we have used it successfully as a laundry tub to rinse everything from small sails to sleeping bags. The tub makes a great temporary storage spot for visitors' duffel bags, a drip-off area for foulies, and a place to safely toss last-minute provisions.

wind routes or live onboard in crowded ports between passages. Keeping clean afloat is a complex problem. Onboard bathing facilities require adequate space and water, should be easy to use and keep clean under way and at anchor, and must be water-efficient.

Shower types

A standard stand-up shower in a head compartment with a shower curtain works, but has some drawbacks. The compartment gets muggy and close-feeling unless there is a hatch ventilating directly into the area. Overspray from the shower and condensation from hot water will cause the enclosed toilet-paper roll to turn soggy, and the overspray must be mopped up afterward. Finally, if the head area is forward of the mast, showering at sea can be difficult, if not dangerous, because of the motion.

So what's the answer? For boats under about 28 feet, one solution is to improve the usual arrangement of the on-deck solar shower by adding a plastic shower enclosure hung from a halyard on the foredeck, or from the boom over the cockpit, to provide windproofing and privacy. Another satisfactory arrangement is to clip a circular shower-curtain ring in the companionway area; the hatch overhead helps things dry quickly after showering and provides ventilation so that condensation is reduced. A small shower pan can be built below the floorboards to contain and direct the water into your sump tank. A small, secure fold-out (or fold-down) seat makes any onboard showering arrangement safer and easier to use.

Water supply

If you have an unlimited water supply or are cruising waterways where freshwater hoses are available, a pressurized cockpit shower works wonderfully for

Spring-loaded on-demand spray nozzles help save precious water

rinsing after a swim and for cleaning feet to keep sand from creeping on board. Unfortunately, pressurized showers consume far too much water on a passage. Unless the water is metered in some way, an unwary bather can use 15 to 20 gallons per shower, and even experienced offshore bathers tend to use 3 to 5 gallons.

Before you set off cruising it is vital to segregate your water tankage so showers can be curtailed before they cause a water shortage. Some sailors close off one tank with sufficient water rations for half the length of a passage; others keep one tank set aside—when it is empty, no more showers. Using a header tank with a limited capacity near and above the shower area will further control usage; pump water up to the header tank and add a kettle of water heated by the galley stove or the engine heat exchanger. Other cruisers use a hand-pump plant sprayer to provide metering and water pressure.

Whatever system you use to supply pressure water, it is most efficient if the bather is seated. A header tank or solar shower bag should be at least 2 feet above the bather to work well. With a pump-type shower sprayer, the bather will need less shower hose and can reach the pump handle more easily from a seated position.

Spray nozzles

Every shower system should have a spring-loaded, on-demand spray nozzle. Because the bather has to hold the lever down, it is easier to save water (on/off push-button nozzles don't work nearly as well). Combining an on-demand spray nozzle with a flexible hose allows the bather to direct water flow efficiently, dramatically decreasing usage. Water usage can be cut further by using a mixer valve, which lets the user set the water temperature, turn the water off temporarily, and then turn it back on at the same temperature.

Water usage

How much water does a water-conscious bather use? On-deck saltwater scrubs followed with a thorough freshwater rinse of body and hair require about 2 quarts of fresh water. With a metered spray-nozzle system, plan on 1 gallon for non-hair-washing showers, 1½ for a two-shampoo-and-cream-rinse shower with short hair, and 2 gallons for long hair. With non-metered systems and bathers who know to wet down, turn the water off, use a small bowl of water for inter-mediate soaping, and use the shower spray only for the final rinse, around 2½ gallons per shower is the norm.

Devoting so much space, cost, and time to perfecting onboard bathing arrangements might seem excessive, but over the past 10 years we've saved 10 times the cost, trouble, and time by being able to choose our destinations and work stops without becoming anchored to shoreside bathing facilities. If a yacht club shower turns out to be utterly luxurious, we can indulge in a long hot soak for pure pleasure, not out of necessity.

VI
FOOD

By Lin and Larry Pardey

FOOD FOR THOUGHT

Lin and Larry Pardey give sea-tried hints for keeping unrefrigerated produce fresh well into an ocean passage

*O*ne potato, two potato, three potato, four; five potato, six potato, seven potato, MORE.

The childhood rhyme was in perfect rhythm with my chore. I would brace myself on "four" as the stern of our 30-foot wooden cutter,

We stock Taleisin *according to the passage length and availability of provisions*

133

Storing Fruits and Vegetables

Some fresh vegetables and fruits can last for extended periods on ocean passages. Proper selection of produce plus proper storage on board are critical. The following guide to storing unrefrigerated produce is based on my records for ocean passages in our two boats and on deliveries of a dozen others. We reserve our cool storage for meats and other special perishables on passages. Our (nonmechanical) icebox has 3 inches of insulation on the sides and 4 inches on the top and bottom. Loaded with six 20-pound blocks of ice, the box will stay cool for 14 to 18 days in the tropics. So far we haven't lacked ice for more than a couple of days on any passage aboard *Taleisin*.

We purposefully are not discussing how to keep fresh meat because it is particularly perishable and must be refrigerated or frozen. We have found butchers in many countries who will vacuum-pack single-meal-size portions of meat. We have successfully kept these packs, unfrozen, up to one month on ice.

We have always been able to keep hard produce unrefrigerated for at least two to three months. Recently, we discovered long-life produce bags, which help keep a larger variety of vegetables and fruits for up to three to four weeks.

The times shown in "Keeping Qualities of Produce" are based on produce that is stored in secure, relatively dark areas of the boat with good ventilation. I have two large baskets that are permanently installed in an open-fronted locker under the stove. On passages these baskets hold most of our onions and potatoes. During a passage I store melons and large squash, nestled in newspaper, in our open-plan chain locker. I store extra produce in newspaper-lined plastic or straw baskets that I wedge securely with cushions and sleeping bags into the forward bunk, an area we don't use while under way. In rough weather it would probably be a good idea to lash down the baskets and tie netting over the open tops to avoid fruit salad in the forepeak.

It is vital to choose a storage area with good air flow and to make sure the baskets are well secured, because bruised produce rots more quickly. If you do not have a free bunk, you can hang produce baskets from the overheads in the forepeak, in an unused forward head compartment, or in the workshop area. You can also hang string hammocks for produce throughout the boat. Be sure that they swing clear of everything—bulkheads, cabinetry, the hull. Otherwise, in rough weather the produce will bruise and rot. Below floorboards and in the lazaret area are my last storage choices, because of poor ventilation.

All produce other than watermelons and hard-skinned squash must be kept absolutely dry. To ensure this, I inspect each item of produce twice weekly and use any that show signs of deterioration.

The preservation times noted in "Keeping Qualities of Produce" are based on buying almost-farm-fresh produce of high quality, which has not been in cold storage and is free of bruises. All times are based on tropical passages.

Taleisin, rose to each trade-wind swell, then I'd relax on "more," as her bow surged upward and a rush of water cascaded along the hull. The potatoes I was counting and inspecting were real—red-skinned, new, Irish, sweet—

Keeping Qualities of Produce

Vegetables	Days in baskets	Days in long-life bags
avocados	14	26
broccoli	2	7
brussels sprouts	4	10
cabbage (large)	40	56
carrots	15	22
green beans (string)	2	7
green peppers (bell)	8	23
leeks	10	21
lettuce (iceberg)	2	7
mushrooms	2	7
onions (brown)	90	not nec.
onions (white)	40	not nec.
potatoes (Idaho, thick-skinned)	70	not nec.
potatoes (new)	100	not nec.
potatoes (sweet, yams)	120	not nec.
squash (hard, such as butternut; also pumpkin)	124	not nec.
tomatoes	20–24*	32*
turnips & parsnips	10	25
Fruit		
apples	10–12	24
cantaloupes	16	not nec.
grapes	3	9
oranges	20	30
tangerines (mandarins)	14	26
watermelons (small)	40	not nec.

*Based on selecting green tomatoes and slowing their ripening by covering

and from a collection of the finest produce I'd ever had onboard for a long passage.

Fremantle, Western Australia, had been a provisioner's heaven at ships' provenders and grocery stores. Australian canned goods competed with Italian, Greek, British, and American specialty items to fill *Taleisin*'s lockers with color and variety.

Best of all, Fremantle had a true farmers' market each weekend. We found Chinese cabbage, spring peas, kale, onions, potatoes, lettuce, and tomatoes, all unwashed, unbrushed, and absolutely fresh. There were also eggs gathered that morning by a farmer who fed his chickens items recycled from his neighbors' stands. This produce would keep for extra days as we sailed to the isolated atolls of the Indian Ocean. When we set off toward Cocos Keeling, five laundry baskets, full to the brim with fruit and vegetables, were

How Much Produce to Carry

Fresh fruit and vegetables are almost always cheaper than their canned equivalents, as well as tastier, more nutritious, and more versatile. They take less storage space than canned goods and require less fresh water to prepare than dehydrated vegetables. So when we prepare for a passage, we overstock on produce, figuring we will lose 10 to 15 percent to spoilage and that it is better and (in most cases) relatively inexpensive to have too much rather than too little. We have found that on tropical islands such as the Tuamotos or Cocos Keeling, simple items such as potatoes and onions that cannot be grown in the climate or soil of coral atolls will cost three to five times more. It pays to overstock on these items before setting sail.

My recommendations for quantities to carry on a passage are based on our style of cooking and eating. Larry and I both prefer a calorie-conscious cuisine, with salads and vegetables for two meals a day and meat, fish, or fowl once a day. We also find that our at-sea lunches—bread, cheese, and fruit or a mixed salad—are more casual than lunches we might eat ashore. We assume that rice and pasta will be substituted for potatoes 50 percent of the time and that one or the other of these starches will form part of our main meal each day.

We recommend that you allow a 50 percent safety margin, in case of a slow passage. Carry at least 15 days' worth of provisions for what should be a 10-day passage, 45 days of provisions for a projected 30-day voyage. The table of quantities (next page) has that margin built in. A good example of why this is necessary is the South African boat we saw arrive in Mauritius under jury rig after having been dismasted. It took the boat 35 days to sail from Cocos Keeling, a passage that most boats complete in 14 to 20 days. The quantities of fresh, unrefrigerated produce in the table below are per person (double the portions for two) based on average appetites.

nestled securely in the forward bunk.

I had selected vegetables and fruits in varying stages of ripeness so they wouldn't all be ready to eat at once. Under way, I have regularly inspected everything for bruises or signs of decay. For eating today I set aside an almost-ripe avocado, some tangerines, two glowing tomatoes, and an onion with the first signs of a green sprout.

During our years of cruising, it hasn't always been as easy to provision. After sailing down the Red Sea in August 1977 onboard our previous boat, the 24-foot cutter *Seraffyn*, it was difficult to find any provisions at all in war-torn Aden, South Yemen. We had depleted our fresh provisions to less than a dozen onions and a half-dozen potatoes, and ahead of us lay 2,200 miles of Arabian Sea. We queried the one remaining ship's chandler (he had only liquor, canned meat pies, and peanut butter), the wife of the manager of BP oil company (who found two dozen precious eggs), and the cook of a freighter impounded in port (he traded a few onions and potatoes for some

Long-lived vegetables[+]	10 days*	Length of Passage 20 days*	30 days*
cabbage (large, 2 lb)	1	2	4
onions (medium, assorted)	7	20	35
potatoes (1/4 lb each, assorted)	8	15	30
potatoes (sweet, yams/small, smooth-skinned)	2	6	15
squash (hard/small, one or two meals' worth each)	1	2	5
Short-lived vegetables[++]			
avocados (different stages of ripeness)	4	7	**
brussels sprouts	2 servings	5 servings	**
carrots (carry extra for snacks)	12–15	25	**
green peppers (bell)	2–4	7	**
leeks	2 servings	5 servings	**
tomatoes (medium)	10	25	**
Fruit[#]			
apples	8	25	**
cantaloupe	1	3	**
oranges (double the amounts for juice)	10	25	**
tangerines (mandarin)	5	10	**
watermelon	1	1	3
Non-produce perishables[##]			
beans & peas, dried (supplement with canned)	none	2 lbs	5 lbs
eggs (fresh, never washed or refrigerated, turn daily to extend longevity)	8	24	40
flour (1/3 whole wheat, 2/3 white, includes bread making)	3 lbs	9 lbs	20 lbs
pasta	2 lbs	5 lbs	8 lbs
rice	2 lbs	5 lbs	8 lbs
yeast	2 oz	5 oz	14 oz

* Quantities per person, 50 percent safety margin included.

** Same quantities as for a 20-day passage; will not last much longer than that.

[+] For long passages, buy long-lived vegetables in quantity because they will last longer and will become your staple fresh food when short-lived vegetable are gone.

[++] In addition to the vegetables listed below, select three or four shorter-lived vegetables such as lettuce, beans, or broccoli; plan on three to six servings per person for each type. This will add variety for the first week of your passage. To extend the life of these perishables, use long-life bags or place these items in cold storage as space becomes available in your refrigeration unit.

[#] Besides the fruit listed below, carry a small selection of softer fruit for the first week of passage. Put these items in your refrigeration unit first as space becomes available.

[##] I stock pasta, rice, and dried beans and peas in generous quantities, even beyond the built-in 50 percent margin, because in an emergency these staples will last much longer than other produce.

wine and yeast).

When we set sail, our fresh provisions barely filled one small wash basin. Yet, when we arrived in Sri Lanka 36 days later, I had two onions left, and Larry and I were in good health. I had learned a dozen new ways to use canned food but admit to being desperate for anything fresh.

Japan presented an interesting contrast when we prepared to sail *Seraffyn*

Long-Life Bags

Long-life plastic bags contain a natural mineral that absorbs ethylene gas; the gas is expelled by fruits and vegetables as a function of maturing and ultimately causes the produce to rot. The Australian bags I used come with instructions for use with refrigeration, but I've found that they also work well without cool storage, providing all produce is absolutely dry before it is stored in the bags. If the produce you buy in the supermarket has been refrigerated, allow it to dry and come up to air temperature for at least 5 or 6 hours in the open away from direct sunlight. If you can find it, however, it's best to buy same-day fresh produce that has never been refrigerated.

We found we can reuse each bag twice if we rinse it well and turn it inside out to dry for at least 10 hours. On our Indian Ocean passage, I waited to rinse the bags until we reached port, to conserve fresh water.

American-made Evert-Fresh bags serve the same function. They're made of mineral-impregnated porous film, which allows moisture to escape and retards the growth of bacteria. Check the company's informative Web site, www.greenbags.com; order by email (thebaglady@greenbags.com); or phone 800-372-3610 for orders and information.

4,600 miles to Canada in 1978. An amazing variety of perfect, fresh produce was beautifully displayed in the local market stalls, but the prices were staggering.

"Apples are a very low price right now," the young Japanese sailor who had offered to translate told me, "only US$2 each. Last month they cost $5." Tomatoes cost $14 a kilo, heads of lettuce $5 each, cabbage about $7 each. From a ship's provender in Tokyo I was able to buy duty-free frozen Philippine prawns at $4 a pound (the locals were paying $16) and Australian beef sirloin at $2 a pound (the local price was $28). But the prices of fresh vegetables, even in quantity, were astronomical.

After much soul-searching, I forked over $400 (in those days six weeks' cruising funds for us) for a carefully considered, but adequate, supply of fresh produce, including an extravagance—24 tomatoes for $56! Imagine my chagrin mixed with appreciation for the gifts we received from Japanese friends during a surprise farewell party—six perfect ears of corn, a gift-wrapped cantaloupe, and, from the yacht club commodore, a case of ripe tomatoes!

Even after 25 years and over 100,000 miles of passagemaking, I often have a bout of anxiety just before Larry and I set sail on a long passage. Did I buy enough provisions? Will there be enough variety? Yet I know my concerns are basically unfounded. With 40 pounds of flour, 20 pounds of rice, 30 cans of meat, 30 cans of fruit, and some condiments, we could get by on a 30-day passage. Add three cabbages, some onions, potatoes, eggs, and apples, and life would be okay.

By replenishing our lockers with canned and packaged goods in the more industrialized countries, we've rarely lacked a varied menu—if I use my imagination. I know this, but still, as I sort through the array of produce from Fremantle, I know that my imagination can rest for the next month. Each day's menu is preordained by the produce that ripens as we rush along with the fresh southeast trades.

By Larry Pardey

STOWAGE SOLUTIONS

Your cruising boat is a warehouse, supermarket, and owner-operated restaurant. Here's how some simple modifications can turn your galley and food-stowage areas cook-friendly

G ood food is a main ingredient of a memorable cruise, and optimiz-
ing your boat's stowage areas means a contented cook—one who
will have more patience for cooking in a seaway. As my grand-
mother used to say, "Always keep on the good side of the cook!" I followed
her advice by building plenty of cook-friendly stowage areas into Lin's and

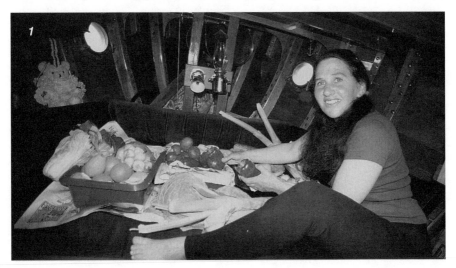

my 29-foot, 9-inch cutter, *Taleisin*.

Two prevoyage challenges face the chef on your boat: Finding places to stow utensils, dishes, and pots and pans so they are easily accessible yet secure and don't rattle in rough seas, and finding spaces in the right places for the food you'll need on the cruise. Neither is much of a problem when you're enjoying local cruising—even 20-foot boats have room for a week's provisions—but setting off on a long cruise can mean stowing the equivalent of two taxiloads of provisions, enough to tax the storage lockers of most boats.

During 30 years of crossing oceans, first on 24-foot, 4-inch *Seraffyn* and more recently on *Taleisin,* and during deliveries on boats ranging from 35 to 85 feet, Lin and I have learned some tricks that can be adapted to expand and reorganize the provisions storage on many cruising boats. The extra provisions you'll be able to carry will both extend your cruising range and save you money.

Take our transatlantic passage on *Taleisin* last year. Before we left England we took on several cases of fine British and Scottish canned meats, desserts, and jams at wholesale prices. In the Madeira Islands we topped up *Taleisin's* "wine cellar" and large forward storage bin with 120 bottles of Portuguese wine at duty-free prices ($1.43 a bottle) plus a case of vintage 10-year-old madeira ($7 a bottle.) So during our three-week stop in Bermuda, a port famous for high prices, we enjoyed luxury provisions imported at bargain prices.

Later, as we cruised the isolated coves of Maine five months out of England, our provisions lockers were still half-filled with European treats. We could choose our destinations not for reprovisioning purposes but because they offered anchorages abundant with shellfish, interesting locals, or perfect serenity.

As you consider storage ideas for galley gear and provi-

sions, remember that stowage that works well in port may not work as well when your boat is rolling downwind, roaring along on a boisterous reach, or sailing to windward at a 20-degree heel. Keep in mind that perishable and packaged foods have different stowage needs too. For example, the nonperishable goods we took on in Porto Santos, an island next to Madeira, had to fit in out-of-the-way places since many of them would not be used for months. However, the fresh provisions had to be readily accessible because we'd need to inspect them three times a week for spoilage. Here's how to tackle the provisions-stowage challenge.

Fresh fruit and veggies. On *Taleisin* we have dedicated storage places for fresh vegetables and fruit sufficient for coastal cruising when we have access to shops every week or two. For ocean passages we store our fresh provisions in large plastic washtubs lined with newspaper (Photo 1) on the forward bunk (we don't use this bunk at sea). The veggies and fruit are out of harm's way and get lots of ventilation. In rough conditions we secure the tubs with a fish net

with four corner lines. The plastic tubs nest together and live in the bilge between passages.

Smart settees. Like many cruising boats, *Taleisin's* port and starboard settees offer the most accessible storage on the boat. To make access easier, we divided each settee cushion into four parts (Photo 2). We lift a cushion seat for direct and full access (the settee's plywood top is part of the cushion bottom) to the storage area we need. We find this type of bin storage provides far more usable space than drawers and is easier to get to and keep clean (as long as we keep it well organized).

Secure buckle-ups. When the weather begins to deteriorate, we buckle up our storage areas (Photo 3); some of the items

stored here are heavy and could hurt the crew in a knockdown. The fore-and-aft strap is made of 1½-inch nylon seatbelt webbing with a quick-release buckle. Since the webbing lies flat, it can be left in place without making the settee uncomfortable to sit on. When the strap is not in use, it takes up little space inside the locker. The strap and buckle came from our sailmaker.

The better bilge. By opening up your boat's floorboards, you can utilize your boat's bilge storage capabilities for everything from a wine cellar to anchor stowage. The bilge aft of *Taleisin*'s maststep is shared by our three-piece, 65-pound Herreshoff fisherman anchor and about six cases of wine (Photo 4). To elevate the bottles above the trickle of water that drains back from the chain locker, we cut plastic industrial antiskid flooring material (the same as used in many engine rooms) to fit.

To keep the cabin safe in a seaway, we made strong floorboard lock-downs of simple barrel bolts and easily fabricated wing nuts. To secure the floorboards in place, we reach underneath and slide the forward and aft barrel bolts into the hole in the adjacent floor beam, then put the center floorboard in place and turn the wing nut to lock it down (Photo 5).

Because we have secure floorboard lockdowns, we are comfortable using our amidships bilge area to store heavy items. In the two 28-inch-long floor bays (Photo 6) aft of the wine cellar/anchor stowage, we store oil, lubricants, and Lin's pet varnish brushes in their pot of kerosene in a strong plastic storage box to ensure that leakage cannot get into the bilge. The box also helps

stored items stay clean. Farther aft we keep two 2½-gallon jugs for extra kerosene and three 5-gallon collapsible water jugs.

Full-access stowage. *Taleisin's* two pilotberths also provide deep bins for provisions. Rather than using plywood tops with small access hatches, we kept every inch of under-bunk area open for storage, courtesy of 8-inch-wide bunkboards of ½-inch-thick cedar (Photo 7). Simple, light, and insect- and mildew-repelling, this arrangement lets us fill the bins to the brim yet have easy access. We line all bins with plastic antiskid material to protect the hull and to stop cans from rattling.

Quiet crockery. To keep our dishes quiet and cushioned in a seaway, we carry a bag of clean sponges and tuck them in where needed (we haven't broken one dish in 15 years!). The cutting board covering the sink (Photo 8) comes in very handy, serving as everything from a serving tray for cheeses to a fish-cleaning platform.

By Tom Wood and Kathy Barron

THE DEPARTMENT OF WATER

When the fresh water runs out, the cruise is over. Liveaboard cruisers Tom Wood and Kathy Barron tell how to clean, filter, and store this precious commodity

I t's easy for urbanites to forget water's importance when a clean, unlimited supply pours forth on demand from the faucet. But cruisers on the move, with limited tankage and facing uncertain sources of supply, are forced to monitor their water closely. Those on their first foreign venture find

Nature's watermaker: A sun tarp equipped with a plastic through-hull fitting at work

Filter and purify (above) all tank water;
change the galley filter (below) regularly

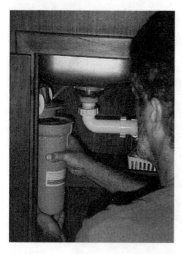

that obtaining safe, potable water and keeping tanks and filters clean can pose problems or unexpected changes in their cruise.

Water hazards

Particulate matter, in the form of small quantities of minerals, dirt, or plant life, imparts an objectionable smell or taste to drinking water. Disease-producing organic life forms, such as bacteria, viruses, and parasites, living in the boat's water tanks can have debilitating consequences. Particulate matter and organic life forms can never be completely eliminated from water, as much of the mineral deposits are totally dissolved, and many life forms are too small to be filtered out. But you can get most of them.

Before taking on water, fill a glass with a sample and inspect it for clarity. Smell and taste it. If it is doubtful, put it in jerry jugs separate from the tank—it can always be used for laundry. If it passes these tests, run the water through a filter before it goes into the tank. We have experimented with many filters and have settled on an ordinary household canister with replaceable activated-charcoal cartridges. These cartridges are widely available, inexpensive, and easy to adapt to almost any setup; they control particles and bacteria down to 2 microns. Our tank-fill filter also functions as a backup to our galley-mounted filter.

It is unwise to skip this filtering process even for rainwater or water from a supposedly secure city supply. All sources can become contaminated. Plant or animal forms growing inside your own hose may be the culprit; don't introduce these cultures into the tank.

Treating the water

Water can be made safe to drink in many ways. Boiling and distillation are always effective. Placing water in a clear plastic bag in direct sun for sever-

Water-Management Strategies

Simple Gifts, our Crealock 37 cutter, carries 80 gallons of water in two tanks. We use a "diversified" approach to managing our fresh water. We track our water use, isolate our water supplies, and utilize different sources for different purposes. Equipment is critical: We use a water catcher, jerry jugs, sun showers, a Seagull filter, and a PowerSurvivor 35 watermaker. Here's how it comes together.

We keep a running tally of our water production and consumption; generally we use 4 gallons of fresh water a day for everything—cooking, drinking, brushing teeth, and rinsing dishes. In a small spiral notebook we keep track of when we last filled our tanks, deduct our daily use, record any additions to our supply, and are thus able to gauge when we need to refill our tank. With the record-keeping system we know when our "water bank" is full and when we can splurge on showers or clothes washing.

We rinse dishes in salt water using the galley foot pump but have found that we get better results if we do the final wash and rinse in fresh water. For convenience we use a 3-gallon jerry jug in the galley and another in the head for washing and filling needs. At approximately 25 pounds, the 3-gallon jug is easier to handle than its 50-pound, 6-gallon cousin.

To give us an easy way to verify each tank's supply, we plan to add a gauge to each water tank by installing a T fitting in the outlet line and running a clear PVC hose from the T up to the vent line on the water tank, securing the hose vertically on a bulkhead where we can read it. Adding 5 gallons at a time to the tank and marking the level on the vertical tube will calibrate the tank level.

Make your own

The PowerSurvivor 35 provides us with 1.4 gallons of pristine water an hour at a price of 5 amps per hour. The watermaker has to be run every seven days, or else the filter must be "inerted" to avoid bacterial growth, which will clog the filter. When we are motoring in clean water, when running the engine at anchor to charge the batteries, and when our Windbugger wind generator is putting out enough power, we turn the watermaker on. Knowing that the output is 1.4 gallons per hour, it is a simple matter to calculate the amount we have added to the tanks by tracking the time the unit is running.

continued on p. 150

al hours destroys many dangerous organisms. Iodine will kill anything that lives in water when added at 2 drops per liter, but the water will acquire an odd taste and some people are violently allergic. A method as old as biblical times calls for mixing wine or other alcohol into the water. The above methods are cumbersome and have other disadvantages, but an emergency may someday make them necessary.

Commercial and pharmaceutical products, in convenient powder or tablet form, are obtainable to purify water. Certain countries, such as Mexico, have approved proprietary products for killing parasites and amoebas endemic to their areas. Use common sense and caution when using these products.

The method preferred by most cruisers to stabilize water is chlorination—

Catching water

I had a sailmaker sew two reinforcing patches into our sun tarp where it sagged when filled with rain, and into the reinforcements I fastened two nylon through-hull fittings with barbed ends. I combined PVC hose and a T fitting to connect the hull fittings together and added a fitting to screw the water-tank fill hose to the rig. When it rains, I let the initial downpour rinse the canvas clean, then direct the hose into the tanks.

Other cruising friends have a deck-mounted fill that allows them to load their tanks by placing a dam of cloth aft of the fill; water coursing down the decks enters the tank rather than flowing overboard. In heavy rains accompanied by lots of wind, the wind can blow the water out of our tarp before it accumulates. When this happens, I block the deck scuppers and use the dinghy pump to suck water off the deck into a bucket, which I transfer into the tanks. On one of our sisterships, the owners have installed a Y valve in the hose leading from the deck scupper to the drain seacock; they close the valve once the decks have washed clean, and the rainwater is routed directly into their tanks.

Shoreside sources

If other water is available, we use it for bathing, dish washing, and laundry and reserve our onboard supplies for drinking and cooking. Instead of showering aboard, we use land-based facilities when available. We also take this approach for laundry; we hand-launder small items on board, using a bucket and a "plumber's helper" as an agitator, and save our major laundry chores for the first laundromat. On *Simple Gifts* our freshwater management allows us to cruise in comfort, knowing that our water supply is safe and ample for our needs.—Jay C. Knoll

adding bleach. Chlorine beach is inexpensive and sold worldwide; it is easy to store on board but must be kept in sealed, opaque containers. Correct proportions are crucial: too little bleach provides false security, and too much is harmful to your health. Any bleach product between 5 percent and 5.5 percent sodium hypochlorite content will work. If the solution is stronger or weaker than this, a little math will work out the proper proportion. Inspect the product label properly to insure that no other active ingredients are included and that no "lemon-fresh" deodorizers or perfumes are present.

Chlorine bleach comes in tablet and powder form—an easy and inexpensive way to carry large volumes—but extreme caution is required in storing and handling this potent oxidizer. If you choose to try the concentrates, read the label closely and calculate the mixtures down to a 5 percent solution with more than due care.

We use two levels of water treatment: "shock treatment" and ongoing treatment. Shock treatment (adding 1 ounce of 5 percent chlorine bleach per 8 gallons of water) insures the death of everything in the tank. This will give the water a distinct "laundry" smell at the tap and also make it slightly slippery to the touch. This water can be used for washing or laundry but *not* for drinking. Pump it through all the lines and taps before disposing or diluting it to a lesser strength. Regular ongoing treatment consists of adding 1 ounce of bleach to every 15 gallons of filtered water. If the water is cloudy or doubtful in any way, we fudge this ratio by rounding up a little. Water treated this way will not taste or smell of bleach and will remain fresh for many months.

Measure the bleach in a glass or plastic measuring cup. Pre-dilute the bleach if necessary, and add water to an empty tank before adding the bleach. If possible, introduce the bleach slowly in conjunction with a stream of water to aid in the mixing process. The addition of more water, along with the normal motion of the boat, will complete the dispersion.

Keeping tanks clean

When jerry jugs are filled from wells, cisterns, or streams, or when rainwater is caught from a deck or awning, minute particles of minerals and debris get into the tanks. In time, muck settles to the bottom of the tank, encouraging blooms of plant and animal life. Tanks on all boats require a thorough scrubbing at least once a year.

Regardless of the material used, tanks must have inspection ports that allow you to reach every surface inside. Even if these openings have been retrofitted, special methods often have to be improvised for cleaning the tanks. For example, if the tanks on your boat are very deep, you may need to use a long-handled mop to reach the bottom.

To clean tanks, drain the water and wipe all inside surfaces thoroughly with a clean cotton cloth soaked in a mild bleach solution. Avoid introducing soap, detergent, or other solvents into the tank. Wipe and rinse repeatedly, removing the rinse water until it is clear without running the dirty water through the freshwater lines and pump.

Inspect the tank for cracks, corrosion, and blisters. A flashlight and mirror are often useful. Inspect all hoses and fittings. Some metal and rubber parts in the pump itself are unavoidable, but all other hoses and piping should be of a plastic material approved for potable water. Clean the strainer in front of the pump, and don't forget the dampening chamber of the pump itself.

Water filters

Stored for long periods, even clean, chlorinated water can acquire an unpleasant taste or odor from the fiberglass, rubber, plastic, or metal parts it touches. To overcome any accumulation of bleach or a "tank taste," drinking water needs filtering one more time before it passes the lips. An independent small tap and filter installed at the galley sink provides a good-tasting, chemical-free supply of convenient H_2O.

Filters come in a wide variety of sizes and costs. Special marine versions are available from General Ecology under the trademarks Seagull and Nature-Pure. We tested one, and it provided exceptional water purity for about one year per cartridge, but the system's cost is high. Household filter canister sets, such as OmniFilter and similar products, are of simple plastic construction and sell at competitive prices through most hardware and home-improvement centers. The filter cartridges are available in several activated-charcoal models that remove taste, odor, and chlorine and are priced between $5 and $10 per cartridge. These elements need to be replaced about every 60 days, but the job takes only a few minutes. Purchase the special wrench and extra O-rings and cartridges at the same time.

Since filters trap all the gunk, holding it in place for disposal later, things soon start to grow inside the cartridge. An odor or taste in the filtered water indicates contamination past the filter. When this happens, remove the cartridge and run diluted bleach through the empty filter canister, hoses, and the tap. Let this solution sit a few minutes before flushing it out with a good run of water, then install the new element.

By Liza Copeland

TRASH: THE DISPOSAL DILEMMA

On a cruise, trash disposal is both an ecological and a practical problem. Here's how to reduce the amount of onboard trash and minimize the impact of its disposal

When stocking up our family's Beneteau First 38, *Bagheera*, in Darwin, Northern Australia, we went to even greater lengths than usual to leave behind as much packaging as possible. Our three young sons helped as we repacked liquids and dry goods into reusable con-

While cruising we use kitchen-size bins in the cockpit locker to separate our metal and glass, paper, and plastic trash

Disposal Methods

U.S. and international pollution guidelines should always be observed. Nothing should be dumped within 3 miles of shore. Outside this limit many goods can be legally dumped as long as they are ground up or cut smaller than 1 inch. Food leftovers, peelings, bones, paper, glass, and metal fall into this category. Although most goods in their raw state can be legally dumped when a boat is more than 12 miles from shore, we consider water depth also and never dump these items in waters shallower than 600 feet. This includes cans and glass containers; both aluminum and steel  cans, contrary to popular belief, take a long time to break down. Bottles and cans thrown overboard in anchorages remain an eyesore for swimmers and may be moved by currents and wave action to the beach. Glass is particularly dangerous. A bottle thrown over the side with the cap on may float for years until it washes up and breaks on the beach. Even without a cap, a bottle can float for weeks and end up ashore.

Cans must be pierced at both ends so they sink immediately. Glass containers should be filled with seawater—easy if you have a saltwater pump in the galley. Bottles can be broken, but this can be hazardous if not done properly. We insert a 24-inch steel bolt through the neck and tap sharply to make the bottom fall out neatly. Plastic, including all forms of rope and foam, must be kept onboard for land disposal. Metallized or plastic-coated cardboard drink cartons, such as those used to package fruit juice, do not break down easily and should be treated as plastic. Although U.S. and international law does permit the dumping of chemicals when over 25 miles offshore, we suggest that all potentially toxic materials be saved for shore disposal. This includes flashlight batteries, paints, old engine oil and filters, medicines, spray cans, and solvents; to keep them safe onboard, place items in sturdy plastic or glass containers.

Just as cities utilize landfills, cruisers must sometimes resort to burying some waste items. The site must be away from the beach and clear of streams and lakes so chemicals cannot seep out and pollute the surrounding area, and the garbage should be buried deep enough to stay buried. Do not bury food scraps with other trash; animals may dig them up. Burying is an option for some materials. While fires create smoke and fumes, on remote islands or in countries that have no appropriate methods of dealing with trash, burning may be the only viable way to dispose of paper, plastics, and, with extreme caution, some chemicals. The fire should be in an isolated location on a beach or other safe area and sited so that smoke, sparks, and fumes are safely dispersed. Fires must be carefully tended, properly put out, and cleaned up afterward by burying the solid residue.

Before You Cruise

When provisioning for a cruise, the amount of trash that will accrue will be greatly reduced by removing unnecessary packaging prior to departure. Items such as flour, rice, cake mixes, breakfast cereals, herbs, and cookies can be stowed in robust airtight and reusable containers. This has the additional advantage of keeping out weevils. In the tropics weevils can quickly infest foods, penetrating cardboard or thin plastic bags to lay their eggs. Cockroaches, also prevalent in the tropics, are less likely to smuggle themselves on board in the folds of cartons and boxes if packaging is removed beforehand. Where possible, buy liquids in glass rather than in plastic bottles. Detergents and cooking oils should be purchased in bulk to last the entire cruise.

Plan engine oil and fuel filter changes in harbors with suitable disposal facilities, even if this means doing it ahead of schedule. Batteries, whether regular or alkaline, contain toxic materials. Use rechargeable nicad batteries for flashlights (a 12-volt charger is necessary) and other gadgets that will accept the slightly lower voltage of these batteries.

tainers. For the next 18 months we would be exploring the islands and atolls of the Indian Ocean, an area with virtually no garbage-disposal facilities.

Since most goods come double-wrapped, hermetically sealed, bubble-packed, or display-boxed, it is essential to reduce the quantity of garbage that will accrue onboard before heading out on a cruise. Even so, disposable material will accumulate on a daily basis and with it the necessity of getting rid of it. How rapidly the issue comes to a head will depend on the number of crew, the size of the vessel, and the climate.

The world's cruising grounds seem vast, and it is all too easy to toss things over the side or dump them behind a bush ashore. Many cruisers still do this, polluting the ocean and beaches. In places as far apart as Madeira, British Columbia's Gulf Islands, and the Maldives, we have come across plastic bags of trash discreetly hidden by passing cruisers. When *Bagheera* was in Turkey, local sailors organized a cleanup to remove such eyesores—and to educate the cruising community. Improper garbage disposal affects not only the environment, but also other cruisers; one of the reasons given by officials in the Seychelles Islands for their strict control over the movements of visiting boats was to reduce damage to reefs and shores.

Plastics are the most pervasive problem. Modern plastics come in a huge variety and have a long life. Even "degradable" plastic bags generally need months of ultraviolet light to start breaking down. Plastic containers can last virtually forever, and if they do break up their effect may be more harmful; many seabirds and turtles die after mistaking small pieces of plastic for food.

Most plastics float (two exceptions are nylon and polyester, commonly used for mooring lines and sheets). Polypropylene, used extensively by commercial and fishing vessels, is very buoyant, and it is not uncommon for cruising boats to become entangled in lost or discarded nets. We witnessed the carnage caused by a large fishing net, covered in goose barnacles and sea growth, that had drifted onto the reef at the entrance to English Harbour, Antigua. Every day dozens of fish became entangled, attracting sharks and barracuda that were in turn trapped. It took several people two days to cut up the net and dispose of it ashore.

Environmentalists argue that everything that isn't quickly biodegradable should be carried aboard until disposal can be made at a shoreside facility. The problem comes on long passages or when cruising in undeveloped areas with no disposal system or one that is not environmentally acceptable. In such cases other means of disposal have to be found. This generally means a compromise between regulations, sound ecological practice, and the reality at hand.

Aboard *Bagheera* we follow a few simple rules. We classify garbage into four categories. Biodegradable materials are those that break down quickly and are absorbed into the ocean—food, leftovers, waste, paper, and cardboard. Metal and glass containers, if disposed of in deep (over 600 feet) water, cause neither visual nor chemical pollution. Plastics are dangerous to sealife and wildlife and can foul propellers and engine cooling-water intakes. Chemicals, such as paint, solvents, and cleaners, require dedicated land-based disposal because of their potentially toxic effect.

Our methods of disposal for the more commonly accumulated garbage are dumping at sea, following the U.S. guidelines, and burial or burning ashore, with great attention paid to the environment and safety. Large items pose specific problems. For example, a cruiser may need to get rid of a sail that is beyond repair, a worn-out inflatable, or a generator or outboard motor that no longer works. These can be disposed of only in proper shoreside facilities.

We are so used to throwing things away that it comes as a surprise that, particularly in developing countries, people often prize the items we discard. In Indonesia we were constantly asked for empty cans and jars; plastic containers were especially sought after. Old books and magazines, old toys and games, even rusty fishhooks and tools, are welcomed by many villagers.

It will take effective international policing to stop all boats from dumping at sea, but we can do our part to improve the situation by employing direct action. Cruising friends of ours in the Caribbean watched angrily as a long line of beer cans drifted from the stern of an opulent yacht. Jumping into his dinghy, Steve collected and returned the cans to their owners, who undoubtedly got the message. As cruising sailors we are privileged to visit some of the most unspoiled and least developed parts of the world, away from the tourist track and the throwaway lifestyle. With some forethought and sensitivity toward the environment, particularly when compromise methods of garbage disposal are the only option, we can preserve our cruising grounds for future generations.

VII FINANCES

By John Kettlewell

MAIL, MONEY, AND MOM

Going cruising for a few months or more but don't know what to do about your mail, bills, bank accounts, and investments? Here's how to stay in touch with family and manage your affairs from afar

Even though we cruisers are bent on escaping the rat race, most of us still need to maintain contact with our relatives and business affairs back home. There are important documents you'll need to receive, whether you're in Bora Bora or cruising the Baja. Even when you're on the move you'll need a permanent address—for example, if you want a telephone credit card or to run a business from your boat—and probably a telephone number or voice-mail box. And to receive mail and messages from family and friends, you'll need a mail-forwarding or a message service. The better organized your connections are to the "real" world, the better your chances of making a great escape.

Organize your mail

A year ahead of your planned departure is not too early to start organizing your mail. Make a list of important mail that arrives on a regular basis, such as credit-card and bank-account statements, tax, boat, and car documents, investment information, insurance, frequent-flyer programs, marine-hardware catalogues, and publications. Don't forget items that arrive infrequently, such as life-insurance premiums and Coast Guard documentation. Note the due dates for important mail, from monthly credit-card bills to yearly or quarterly income taxes, and mark a calendar with the arrival date of upcom-

Web Commerce and Mail

AT&T: www.att.com
American Express:
www.americanexpress.com
Bear Stearns & Co.:
www.bearstearns.com
Blue Mountain:
www.bluemountain.com
BOAT/U.S.: www.boatus.com
Defender Industries:
www.defenderus.com
Federal Express: www.FedEx.com
Fidelity Investments: www.fidelity.com
Hallmark Cards: www.hallmark.com
Hotmail: www.hotmail.com
Juno: www.juno.com
JSI The Sailing Source:
www.sailnet.com/store/
Landfall Navigation:
www.Landfallnav.com
Macy's: www.macys.com
Merrill Lynch: www.merrilllynch.com
The New York Times:
www.nytimes.com
Charles Schwab: www.schwab.com
USA Today: www.usatoday.com
West Marine: www.westmarine.com
Yahoo!: www.yahoo.com

ing bills or license renewals (I also keep a file on my computer to help remind me). Knowing when your bills will arrive will be handy when planning a mail drop—you'll probably be able to get most of your important mail in one shot.

Reduce your mail load

Cancel unneeded mail before you go cruising—subscriptions, memberships, and the like (I also canceled my car registration). The more deletions you make, the more manageable your mail load becomes. Be ruthless with magazines, because their weight can add significantly to your postage bills. Next take a look at eliminating, consolidating, and simplifying the handling of your bank accounts, credit cards, and taxes. Do you need two checking accounts and two savings accounts? You might if you are self-employed and will be managing your business from onboard. Can you consolidate your spouse's accounts with yours? Can you arrange to have a certain amount of money transferred from your savings account to your checking account at selected intervals?

The "simplify" part of this equation can be very helpful. For instance, the IRS and my state tax department will deposit tax refunds electronically. Charges on the AT&T Universal Card, MasterCard debit card, and Discover Card I use are automatically debited from my checking account.

If you can't arrange to have your bills paid automatically, appoint someone reliable to take care of them. The postal service outside the cities in many cruising areas is too slow and unreliable to count on receiving bills or important documents in a timely manner. I once missed a perfect weather window for the rough upwind passage from the British Virgin Islands to St. Maarten because I was waiting for mail to arrive. When my air-mail package showed up three weeks late, I had run out of time and had to skip some wonderful cruising.

Cyber-Mail, Cyber-Management

Like islands and anchorages, cyber cafés, copy centers, and mail-service outfits that provide Internet access are scattered across many popular cruising areas. With an Internet connection you can access your checking, investment, and some credit accounts as well as send and receive email. You won't need to wait for "snail mail" to know your bank accounts' current balances, the prices of your securities, or to pay your phone or credit card bills. You can take advantage of free email from Hotmail and Yahoo!, among others, and send free or low-cost cyber-greeting cards via Hallmark and Blue Mountain arts.

Most of these services also provide computers and printers, so the only reason to dinghy your laptop ashore is to use AOL or plug your modem into a public phone. During the past year of cruising the Pacific I've been able to spend an hour online, taking care of business back home, for US$3 to $10.

Online checking and stock trades

My husband, Matt Rollberg, and I have an Ultra Service Account (USA) at Fidelity Investments; the services include a VISA debit card for ATM withdrawals (fees are quite low), checking, money transfers to and from other bank accounts (though not electronically), and brokerage services. I can get my account statement from Fidelity's Web site, including recent ATM withdrawals and checks cleared. I also get financial information from a variety of sources and make trades online through Fidelity. Before you leave home, find out what services your primary brokerage service and bank offer; electronic banking, reporting, account trading, and discount brokerage are those you want in place.

In far-flung ports newspapers can be as scarce as the albatross; in Suva, Fiji, for example, a several-weeks-old *USA Today* sells for about $5—if you can find one. I've enjoyed getting the news online from *The New York Times* and *USA Today* as well as my local paper and favorite magazines.

Online credit-card, mail, and shopping services

You can check on your credit-card and phone accounts with AT&T and American Express, among others, online.

Shopping online can save cruisers a lot of legwork. For example, when our laptop died I was able to research various models and chose a replacement, which I bought in Australia. Online shopping is a real convenience, since most sources will ship your purchase to any address. For example, last Christmas in Australia we sent gifts to family and friends in the States from Macy's, which offers a gift registry and 250,000 products as well as shipping. Some marine-hardware suppliers, such as BOAT/U.S., Defender, JSI, Landfall Navigation, and West Marine, sell and ship products through their Web sites.

Onboard cyber-connections

Using the Inmarsat system on our boat to send email or to fax documents through our service provider, COMSAT, costs about $10 for each one-sentence message and $25 for a full paragraph. COMSAT charges one cent per digit, including spaces, empty lines, and punctuation; they also have a standard format that substantially adds to the cost of the message. On the other hand, if you're cruising an area with no or limited phone service, the ability to make contact by email through Inmarsat can be worth every penny. I've used Inmarsat to place trades with my broker. However, the confirmation, with routine disclaimers, runs $25 to $30. Fidelity does not accept Inmarsat (non-Internet) email to trade stocks or transfer money.

Online systems that interface with single-sideband radios, such as ham radio packet communications, Software Systems Consulting's P-Sea Mail, and PinOak Digital's PODLink, are a lot less expensive than Inmarsat. However, propagation problems can interfere with sending and receiving, and the system's geographic reach may not cover the area you'll be cruising. We tried to integrate P-Sea Mail with our ICOM 700 single-sideband only to learn, after a frustrating month, that the software works only with the ICOM 710. The advantage of Inmarsat is that you can communicate virtually instantly and when you want to. COMSAT also provides comprehensive international news for free, which means you won't use up any battery power listening to the BBC or Voice of America on the single-sideband.—Margaret Reichenbach

Special handling

The annual renewal form for Coast Guard documentation will be sent to the address on the document, so be sure to notify the Coast Guard of your address changes. However, you can request an early-renewal form from the Coast Guard, and your agent can sign your name and return the form. For the latest info contact a private documentation service or the National Vessel Documentation Center at 800-799-8362.

Many states require an annual payment of registration fees, excise tax, and/or property tax for your boat (however, this tax will apply only if you are in state waters for more than 90 days; some states have different grace periods).

Many states now offer five-year (or longer) renewals for driver's licences, which reduces but doesn't eliminate the hassle of renewing this important document. Some states allow renewals by mail, though most require a new photograph and an eye test at each renewal. Check with your state motor-vehicle bureau to see if you can renew before setting off.

Establishing a home address

For most mail a post-office box, where your mail will be safe (should, for example, your mail-forwarding service fail to pick it up), works well. (If you choose to use a mail-forwarding service, its address will likely become your "home" for legal and financial purposes.) But check that your state allows a post-office box to be used when applying for a driver's license, rather than a street address. Consider, too, whether you'll need a street address for UPS and Federal Express deliveries, packages from mail-order firms, and for voter registration.

If you decide to move your mailing address to another state, you may have to prove to the tax collectors that you've changed your domicile. One way is to open bank accounts in the new area, get new driver's licenses, and register to vote. It took years of letters, phone calls, and faxes to get my boat off South Carolina's property-tax rolls when I changed my domicile to Maine. Maine's tax guide defines domicile as follows: "Domicile is where you intend to make your permanent home. An individual can have only one domicile or permanent home for tax purposes. (Domicile is the home where an individual has the most legal ties.)"

If, however, you want to maintain ties to your former hometown, retain your former domicile (in terms of bank accounts and voter registration). This minimizes hassles with license renewals and unfamiliar local regulations and tax codes (and means you'll be contributing to your local community and state tax base). Where you maintain your domicile might also be important if you plan to home-school your kids on the boat. Regulations on home schooling vary tremendously by state; for instance, New York requires the administration of standard tests at certain intervals.

Mail forwarding and receiving mail

Some professional mail-forwarding services specialize in providing cruisers with a "home base," including a street address and a telephone number. They will transcribe messages and put them in your next mail package, or you can call in (sometimes on a toll-free line). Some mail services also provide voice mail, single-sideband radio messaging, and bill paying.

If a friend or member of your family volunteers to sort and forward your mail, accept the offer only if they are enthusiastic about taking on the responsibility. Otherwise the job will become a chore and won't get the attention it needs.

Once you've finalized your mail-delivery arrangements, I suggest planning on receiving mail twice a month maximum in the U.S. Postal Service range and once a month maximum when overseas. Don't use a preset schedule of mail drops, because it's not practical to follow an itinerary on a sailboat. It's better to notify your mail-forwarders after you arrive in port. Mail within the United States should be addressed to "General Delivery" (and to "poste restante" when overseas) in small or medium-size towns. Don't have your mail sent general delivery to a large city; you'll likely spend a long time tracking down your package. To avoid confusion, use your last name only in the address: Smith, Yacht *Peregrine* (Hold for Arrival), General Delivery, City, State, Zip Code, Country. Shipping services such as Federal Express, UPS, and DHL are often the fastest and most reliable way to ship to overseas addresses.

Receiving mail while you're cruising is always fun—reading about that ice storm back home, getting a look at your friend's or relative's baby, or catching up on the latest hometown gossip. The key to keeping mail fun instead of a burden is to organize, reduce, and prioritize your mail before you go.

By Robin Lutz Testa

CUSTOMS CLEARANCE

Whether you're cruising Bahrain or the Bahamas, when you check into a foreign port the right attitude, papers, and procedures will help you clear in and out easier and faster

E ntering ("clearing in") and exiting ("clearing out") a foreign port is regarded by many cruisers as an arcane process. Although most countries monitor and control who enters and exits, as well as what visitors bring with them and what they take out, clearance procedures for cruising boats vary widely from country to country—and often, from port to

Elizabeth Wrightson

Customs kit: Previous clearance papers, passport photos, and ship's stamp help speed clearing in

Clearing-In Questions

When you clear in, asking the following questions will help clarify a country's or a port's particular requirements:
- What must be done to cruise these waters—do I need to obtain a cruising permit, keep a transit log, or clear in and out of every port?
- How long may my crew and I stay in the country? How do we renew our visas?
- How long and under what circumstances may my boat stay in the country without incurring duty?
- What must I do if I want to leave my boat here and fly home or to another country?
- What must I do if I make crew changes?
- What is the procedure for purchasing duty-free diesel, spirits, and other goods?
- What is the procedure for clearing out?

port. In some areas it can be hard to find anyone who cares that you've arrived, while in others requirements are very strict, and some officials make a cottage industry out of clearing cruisers in and out.

But doing some homework (embassies, consulates, and travel guides are good sources of information) on what is required to enter a particular port or country, such as whether visitors' visas must be obtained beforehand or can be issued on arrival, and preparing yourself with the right documents, information, and questions will minimize problems. And when dealing with clearance officials, a generous amount of patience (smaller ports and some countries run on "island time") and respect (inappropriate dress, such as bare feet, swimsuits, short shorts, or rubber sandals, is discourteous) will help things go smoothly.

Clearing-in procedures

Just as aircraft from overseas may land only at an international airport, a cruising boat entering a foreign country must make its first stop at a designated "port of entry" (listed in pilot books). Although there are exceptions, when you enter a country's territorial waters it is illegal to anchor or go ashore anywhere but a port of entry. In addition to flying your national flag, fly the country's courtesy flag uppermost from your boat's starboard spreader and hoist the "Q" (yellow) flag to indicate that everyone aboard is healthy and that you request *pratique*—permission to land. Also, call port control on VHF channel 16 for entry instructions; if you don't get a response, only the skipper may go ashore to find officials and request *pratique*. You may save money by waiting for normal business hours; there often are overtime charges for clearance after hours or on a weekend or a holiday.

Technically, until you are granted *pratique* no one and nothing can leave or come aboard your boat; some officials are lax about this and others are

When You Need an Agent

In countries where bribery/baksheesh is known to be an inescapable part of the clearance process, employing a customs-clearance agent can keep you at arm's length from the practice. Apart from using an agent, we have heard of a number of other ways of dealing with overt or implied demands by officials for money and for negotiating clearance procedures in countries where baksheesh or "tips" are part of the social fabric.

One cruiser we know successfully uses the "stupid strategy"—he feigns profound incomprehension, causing the official to give up in disgust and concentrate on his next, presumably easier, prey. Another cruiser uses the "friends in high places" strategy—he drops the name of a highly placed local acquaintance and mentions how displeased this person would be when told about the difficulty. There is also the "I'm in no hurry" strategy: one cruiser who used

this tactic somehow got permission to tour the countryside while his clearance (which was in the hands of an agent) dragged inconclusively on. After two weeks and still no clearance, he was told to leave the country, which by then was fine with him. Another cruiser simply refused to pay what he considered an improper "fee." His boat was impounded, but, with help from his consulate, he got it back. Lastly, the "just don't go there" strategy, while it may limit your cruising, is an effective way to avoid what Americans think of as corrupt officials.

We have found that in most countries and ports clearing in and out is usually a straightforward process, and that most officials are as courteous and efficient as circumstances permit. Whatever your clearance experience, make sure that your behavior leaves a clean wake for the cruisers who will follow you.

strict, but avoid discovering which the hard way. Usually, you will be required to check in with the following authorities:

Immigration/police will inspect your passports to verify that you and your crew may legally enter the country and will tell you how long and under what circumstances you may stay.

Customs will determine the duty status of your boat and its equipment and goods (especially liquor, tobacco, drugs, firearms, and ammunition) and place under bond any controlled items, such as firearms, spearguns, excess liquor, and banned literature. Failing to declare such items places you at risk of penalty or imprisonment and your boat in danger or confiscation.

Quarantine/health/agriculture will check the health of your crew and determine if any prohibited or controlled foods, plants, pets, or other materials are aboard. Prohibited items will be seized; controlled items may be held in bond. Pets may be subject to quarantine.

Port captain will check your boat's registration and the clearance certificate from your previous port.

If you are lucky, all of these functions will be vested in one official or in representatives of each authority either able to visit your boat or located close to the anchorage. In some ports, however, you'll have to travel from one office to the next and back again—we try to look at it as a way to get some exercise and become acquainted with the town.

Documents and information

Before your clear in, consider what documents and information about your boat, crew, and equipment you may need to complete the clearance process, especially if the port is a "travel all over town" situation. Clearing in will go faster when you're prepared. If you're going to spend only a couple of days in the country, it may be possible to clear in and out at the same time; ask about this possibility when you arrive.

Materials: Bring ballpoint pens, a supply of blank paper, at least five sheets of carbon paper, and your ship's stamp. While a ship's stamp isn't a necessity, it will save you some time and may represent a certain amount of authority for some officials. At a minimum, the stamp should carry your boat's name and home port. Clearance officials in poor or developing countries may not have adequate paper, much less typewriters, computers, or photocopiers—but it is often just these places that require the greatest amount of paperwork. After you have filled out several forms in quintuplicate, you'll appreciate bringing your own carbon paper.

Documents: Bring the passport of each crewmember, your boat's registration (U.S. Coast Guard documentation is preferred over a state registration), the clearance certificate form from your previous port, and a crew list with each crewmember's name as it appears on his or her passport, nationality, and position on the boat ("crew" will usually suffice). Leave space on the crew list to add other information that officials may require. If an official asks you to make photocopies of any of your documents, make a few extra—other officials may want copies too.

Information: It's a good idea to have papers, such as your radio operator's and firearms license, insurance documents, your pet's international health certificate, and a letter or prescription from your doctor detailing medicines on board (especially narcotics and prescription drugs), at the ready. But remember that, unless asked, you needn't volunteer this information. Even then, a general answer is often sufficient—even welcome. For example, when we are asked about prescription drugs, stating "ship's pharmacy" usually proves acceptable.

Because you may be asked for additional or specific information about your crew, your boat, or your boat's equipment, compiling a checking-in "data sheet" can save time and trips back to the boat to chase down information. Crew information should include: each crewmember's full name and nationality; passport number, place and date of issue, and date of expiration; place and date of birth; occupation and residential address; and the names and contact details of next of kin. Information about your boat should include: length, beam, and draft (in both feet and meters); displacement (in registered net and gross tons); number of masts and type of rig; hull material; hull, deck, and cabinhouse color; sail color and sail number; engine make, type, horsepower, and cruising range and speed under power; fuel and water capacity; life-raft capacity and date of last service.

A few countries require a list of your boat's equipment detailing the item, manufacturer, model number, and serial number. Usually this covers radios (including hand-helds), navigation equipment (GPS, radar, RDF, and weatherfax), safety equipment (EPIRB and life raft), personal electronics (computer, video equipment, stereo, and cell phone), and camera equipment and binoculars. Remember, having detailed information on your boat, crew, and equipment doesn't mean that you must volunteer it.

In some countries the clearance process is so labyrinthine (see "When You Need an Agent"), or language is such an obstacle, that it may be standard practice to hire an agent. Check with other cruisers or cruising guides to find an agent who is reliable and fair.

Clearing-out procedures

Before you and your boat leave the country, clearance officials (usually the port captain) may require that you notify them of your departure date and leave from a designated port of entry. When planning your departure, take into account the day of the week (clearing out may not be possible if official offices are closed) and make sure you allot enough time for the clearance process and to retrieve the goods held in bond or make duty-free purchases. Usually, although not necessarily in this order, you will need to visit the following officials:

Immigration/police will stamp your documents and refund any departure bond you have posted.

Customs will make arrangements for duty-free purchases and record the departure of your vessel.

Port captain will collect any port fees and issue a certificate of clearance, which will show your intended departure date. Technically, you must leave on that date, although officials in some ports are not strict about enforcement. If your exit is delayed, you should notify the port captain, who may require you to clear in and out again. When a port of entry is located far from the country's territorial limit, as is often the case with countries consisting of many islands, or you wish to stop at a country's outer islands after clearing out, inquire about such arrangements before clearing out.

By Lin and Larry Pardey

MONEY MATTERS

What's the best way to have money transferred from home? How do you avoid high fees when exchanging currency? Should you carry cash, traveler's checks, or credit cards? Lin and Larry Pardey look at how to deal with money in remote parts of the world

One aspect of world cruising that has become simpler and less costly since Larry and I first began voyaging 25 years ago is dealing with money. With the advent of electronic banking and international credit-card services, we've found that receiving our twice-yearly supply of cruising funds, even in remote parts of the world, takes a tenth the time it once did. But being prepared for the various situations you'll face as you cruise internationally does require forethought. You not only have to get your hands on the money you have back home, but you also need to ensure that you have money for your first days in a new port.

Cashing in

It's almost impossible to arrive in a new country with a prepurchased supply of local cash, since few banks carry anything but a small bit of their nearest neighbors' currency. The best solution we've found is to carry a stash of U.S. traveler's checks (about $2,000) in small denominations plus some U.S. cash (about $500) in small bills to cover our immediate needs and for use in case of emergency.

Small denominations work best in places where there are no banks and the cash reserves of the average store are small. We have found U.S. currency to be the easiest to change—with British pounds second and German marks third—and to use, even in places that don't accept traveler's checks. Speaking of traveler's checks, some issuers, such as American Express, offer checks that two people sign when purchasing but require only one signature when cashing.

Where to exchange money. In countries with stable, internationally convertible currencies, banks usually give the best exchange rates; hotels and private currency-exchange services may take commissions as high as 5 percent. Buy and sell rates should be posted.

We initially change only enough money to take us out for dinner our first night in port, since we find the rates are often less good near a harbor. Then we check among local sailors, at banks, and with businessmen. Until we know the ropes, we change money where we see rates posted and can get a receipt; some countries have strict laws against changing money except at authorized dealers, and countries with currency controls require exchange receipts for reconversion at departure time. Using branches of the same bank for all your transactions will make it easier to confirm your currency claims when you leave the country.

We have occasionally sold currency to black-marketing locals, but only where this is very common practice and the penalty for a first-time offense is a warning. In some countries you may forfeit your boat and spend time in jail if caught, so find out first what risks are associated with nonbank money transfers. The foreign-exchange official at a major big-city bank can be a very good source of information.

Fees. Before you transfer funds, exchange money, or open a local bank account, ask about fees. These can differ from bank to bank or even from from branch to branch; one may have no transaction fee, another a charge per check, yet another a single fee for changing as many traveler's checks as you wish.

Dealing with inflation. In general, you'll save on transaction fees by changing enough money to last at least a week at a time, or longer if you're going to travel around the country. But if you're planning to spend some time in a country where inflation is high, you'll need a different strategy, since you'll lose money at the end of your stay if you have to reconvert local currency you bought earlier when the value was higher.

Practical tips. Choose a quiet time at the bank to make all but the smallest transactions, being careful to avoid local paydays. And be as careful with your cash in a foreign city as you would be in any U.S. city: Don't put your cash in pants pockets, don't put your wallet on the counter when you're shopping, and watch out for pickpockets who hang out around banks. Women without a male escort should be especially careful when changing money.

It's best to carry only as much money as you need for the day or for shopping. Consider carrying a change purse with just enough cash for the purchases you'll make in the local market. Keep extra cash separately in a safe spot on your person, and recharge your change purse in private. Visible cash could encourage market prices to go up.

Buying a car

We decided to purchase a 4X4 *bakkie* (pickup truck) for a photo safari when we arrived in Durban, South Africa. We had the funds with which we purchased the vehicle transferred to the First National Bank, which has branches throughout the country. For the rest of our stay, we found it easy to do our banking at any of these branches. When we sold the 4X4, we readily changed our rand back to dollars using the same bank chain.

If you've bought a local vehicle for touring, don't keep it until the last moment. Sell it a month or two before you depart and use the funds for provisioning and refitting. We've seen too many vehicles abandoned by cruisers who used them too long and then didn't have time to sell them.

Money transfers

Credit cards. For transferring large amounts of money to buy provisions and traveler's checks, we've found that nothing beats a major credit card. Over the past 10 years, in 14 countries, we've done 90 percent of our money transfers by credit card at almost no cost and with immediate service. To eliminate interest charges, we prepay the advance by sending a check to our account about three weeks before we want to request funds. We then go to a resort town or large city and ask for a cash advance at a bank that handles Visa. Even though the card has a credit limit of $5,000, we can draw up to the amount of our deposit, usually at a cost of only $2 (some foreign banks have charged a small service fee for larger cash amounts). The only drawback is that the bank will issue funds in local currency, which we must then exchange for the currency in which we wish to purchase traveler's checks.

ATMs. Automated teller machines (ATMs) work for cash advances up to about $150 per day. You pay the normal $2 fee. The drawback is that the exchange rate on these smaller transactions is less favorable than on large cash advances.

Telex. A telex transfer, which requires written authority sent to your home banker, is far more costly than a cash advance—according to our information, a $40 fee for the transfer at the originating end and up to 1 percent of the total amount at the paying end. You also have to allow up to four days for clearance from the date your bank wires the funds. To use telex transfers, send your bank two separate letters stating the amount you want (to help guarantee that at least one will get through) and include the name, address, and branch of the bank you'll be using, plus its Swift number (telex code). Be sure to direct the telex transfer to the recipient who is most likely to go to the bank.

Other instruments. Letters of credit work only in large cities and sometimes require collateral. Cashiers or banker-trust checks must be drawn on a well-known bank and have two official signatures; we've found that the banks whose checks are most likely to be accepted include Bank of America and New York Trust in the United States, National Westminster or Barclays in the United Kingdom, and West Pac in Australia and New Zealand.

Faxes. Before you set sail, arrange with your bank manager at home to accept a fax signature for emergency transactions or to verify the requests of whoever is handling your financial affairs in your absence. Fax machines are available in the most remote islands in the world. Although many banks will tell you they cannot accept fax signatures for fund transfers, with a little persuasion our home-base New Zealand bank manager arranged a special code to allow us to do just that in an emergency.

Strategies. If you're cruising in a less-developed area or requesting funds in excess of $10,000, you may find there is a week or two delay while the bank clears the telex or draft. We plan our twice-yearly refunding stop to coincide with a haulout and refit so that the messy work and the delays occur together.

We know of no way to avoid spending money on currency exchange. It costs us about $300 a year in exchange differences, charges, and traveler's check purchase fees. Traveler's checks are worth the investment, though, because of the ease of replacing them if they are stolen or lost. Furthermore, the 1 percent you pay to purchase these checks will be regained when you exchange them for foreign funds, as the rates for traveler's checks are up to 1½ percent higher than for cash.

You'll need your passport and other forms of identification to get a refund for lost traveler's checks. For security we have made color copies of all relevant pages of our passports and of our driver's licenses; we pasted them on thin cardboard and carry these copies with us. We carry the original passports only when a bank requires them, and then we leave the copies on board for security.

Two final notes: Small foreign shipyards have had some poor experiences with cruising sailors. Offer to leave a deposit before you start using their facilities, and then run a tab.

Lastly, spend any coins before you leave for a new country, or toss them in a jar to give to other sailors going the opposite way. Money changers won't accept foreign coins, but cruisers find a gift of coins for their next port of call a pleasant windfall.

By Julie Palm

A MID-CAREER SABBATICAL

Rick and Julie Palm explain their plan for circumnavigating while keeping career opportunities open for their return

W hen Rick and I married in 1980, we both had successful careers, and we both had a 10-year plan—to sail around the world. We envisioned a circumnavigation not as a retirement lifestyle, but as a mid-career sabbatical. We wanted to start when we were young enough—

Sojourner *begins Rick and Julie Palm's mid-life adventure*

Onboard Cruising Expenses (Europa Legs, U.S. $)

	Cyprus	Egypt	Sudan/ Djibouti	Thailand	Sri Lanka	Malaysia	Singapore
Communications	318	111	88	103	107	15	68
Restaurant meals	297	857	466	501	138	136	241
Transportation	110	54	25	479	3	28	50
Customs/immigration/ port fees/tips	40	239	97	55	7	–	5
Marina fees/ race entries	344	72	–	200	–	165	–
Food	627	150	316	423	343	108	351
Boat parts/services	1,981	–	264	1,751	124	130	444
Fuel/dinghy, gas/propane	138	193	180	262	45	130	85
New clothing/ laundry/haircuts	55	–	3	25	14	11	60
Entrances fees/ tours	46	1,080	118	–	37	2	–
Gifts/books/ USA parties	7	160	–	235	–	36	152
Photography	36	–	–	4	–	–	12
Finance charges	31	–	–	81	–	–	–
Hotels	–	100	116	291	–	–	–
Fishing/dive expenses	–	–	–	58	–	–	–
Miscellaneous	31	–	–	93	–	–	–
Total	**4,061**	**3,016**	**1,673**	**4,561**	**818**	**761**	**1,468**
Per month (20 months) avg. per mo.	–	–	–	–	–	–	–
People on board	2	4	4	3	4	4	3

The table above is a breakdown of our expenses during 20 months of cruising in 1991–92, including participation in most of the Europa 92 rally. By many cruisers' standards the totals are high because: we completed many of our commissioning projects while under way, after we left New York and prior to leaving the Caribbean; boat expenses for our 35,000-mile circumnavigation, which normally might be spread over several years, were condensed into 20 months; and with limited time for land travel, we often used more-expensive modes of transportation and organized tours.

44 and 42—to handle the physical requirements of the voyage. We also wanted to return two to four years later and reenter the work force with time to recoup our finances before retirement (or the next 10-year plan, whichever came first). We began to build a plan, adopting concepts foreign to many cruisers but realistic for us and, we suspect, for many people who don't want to cruise for the rest of their lives.

We realized that, in order to complete our goal, we would have to accept some restrictions and compromises. Since we would have to cruise on a schedule, we decided to participate in the Europa 92 Round-the-World Rally,

Onboard Cruising Expenses (Europa Legs, U.S. $)

Bali	Australia	Vanuatu	Fiji	Tonga	French Polynesia	Panama	Caribbean	New York/ Norfolk	Total
20	127	–	64	33	63	72	296	9	1,494
432	496	280	294	376	701	55	546	121	5,937
48	86	2	44	11	180	98	153	6	1,377
2	70	–	21	–	–	61	139	–	736
–	–	–	12	–	–	88	437	117	1,435
322	1,008	173	544	629	1,188	600	1,451	1,749	9,982
116	722	–	1,519	35	2,652[3]	790	3,899[4]	1,765	16,192
122	466	136	355	409	464	153	531	208	3,877
52	47	133	38	23	119	7	461	25	1,073
96	–	–	30	28	5	70	43	–	1,555
171	242	121	78	13	15	93	250	66	1,639
–	–	–	2,130[2]	69	54	–	127	–	2,432
–	245	–	–	–	–	–	86	60	503
174	539	–	202	–	–	–	–	–	1,422
250	2,189[1]	113	23	43	114	174	980	–	3,944
–	292	9	–	–	–	–	86	60	571
1,805	6,529	967	5,354	1,669	5,555	2,261	9,485	4,186	54,169
–	–	–	–	–	–	–	–	–	2,708
4	3	3	4	4	4	4	3	3	–

Note: includes (1) new compressor, (2) new camera, (3) new spinnaker, (4) new dinghy

A Buddhist shrine in Sri Lanka

whose 15-month itinerary became part of our plan and whose organizational support helped us finish the voyage. We wanted to see the world, as well as sail around it. To circumnavigate on a schedule and travel on land, we would have to plan a higher budget than many long-term cruisers.

Making the decision to take a mid-career sabbatical meant giving up some of the advantages of a more permanent cruising life. We looked with envy, for instance, on

Expenses at Home (20 Months, U.S. $)

Furniture storage	3,700
AT&T phone bills	2,237
Boat insurance	7,814
Mail forwarding/newsletter distribution	2,209
Rally fees (Caribbean 1500 + Europa 92)	8,215
Medical expenses for dependents at home	1,173
Accountants fees/tax filings	1,771
Memberships/subscriptions/charitable contributions	2,674
Total	**29,793**
Per month	**1,490**

Rick catches a dolphin fish almost his size

our friends in Thailand who stayed there several seasons, long enough to get involved with the community and teach English to a group of young Thai girls. As part of the 30-boat Europa 92 fleet, we often overwhelmed some of our hosts in small island countries. When our rally participants had eaten every egg on the Galápagos Islands, we wished for a more solitary trek through Darwin's paradise. We had looked forward to the much-acclaimed diving in the Red Sea. But when heavy weather was unrelenting, our schedule did not allow us to take shelter and wait for calmer seas and opportunities to dive. At times, we were forced to have parts air-shipped to us in order to make the start of the next leg, rather than waiting for shipment via a less-expensive method.

While at times the compromises were frustrating, we look back on our adventure and easily conclude that, for us, the trade-offs were worth it. The fact that we returned to the working world as excited about working as we were when we left it two years before proves that, for us, a scheduled trip with a scheduled return was the way to go.

Very early on in our planning stages, we made a habit of "putting the plan first." To some, our financial planning may have seemed shortsighted, because we emphasized saving enough money to go sailing after 10 years instead of saving for retirement.

Our definition of our post-high-school parenthood role was also foreign

Grand Totals (per Couple, U.S. $)

20 months, onboard	31,095*	12 months, onboard	18,657
20 months, at home	29,793	12 months, at home	17,876
Total	**60,888**	**Total**	**36,533**

* Lower figure than onboard expenses table total, because onboard expenses were figured for average 3.5 people onboard per leg. This table figures per couple.

to many. We gave my son, Ted, now 20, the choice of taking time out between high school and college to join us or of going directly to college. If he chose (as he eventually did) to start his freshman year at Kenyon College in Ohio right after high school, he knew we would not be close enough to help him emotionally. I watched with pride as he exerted his independence while also building a support structure with relatives in Ohio.

Although we were a two-career family, saving took special care. We needed to save not only for the voyage, but also for Ted's education and for reentry if we were faced with the very real possibility of not being able to sell the boat when we returned.

Rick's past experience as a stockbroker gave him some special skills to work with our investments, sometimes in difficult economic times. We invested conservatively, knowing that once we were at sea, we would not be close enough to market information to make timely decisions. Bonds, maturing at critical times to support our schedule, were a key part of our financial plan.

I was able to defer part of my income from my last year at work in order to stay on the payroll at a very modest level during our absence. This income did not contribute significantly to the voyage, but it allowed the medical coverage for us and Ted to continue.

Boat insurance was a requirement of the Europa 92 Rally and something we also wanted. But quotes from many U.S. companies exceeded our budget. We were able to get the coverage we needed within our budget from a French company (PME Assureur in Hyères).

We had stayed in the same house I had bought before Rick and I were married, so our house mortgage was small. We sold the house and most of our furniture before we left to help finance the voyage and to give us flexibility in relocating when we returned. Our cars were modest. By choice, sailing was our major and, in the summer our only, entertainment.

We had several boats before we settled on our Tayana 52 for the voyage. Because our plan entailed a schedule, we needed a boat that could sail at reasonable speed with a shorthanded crew. *Sojourner* met our needs so well that we plan to keep her until we complete our next 10-year plan and go cruising again.

Sailing on a schedule meant special preparation for anticipated maintenance on the boat and as much self-sufficiency as possible. At many stopovers we would not have time to send for parts, nor would we be able to find and schedule workmen. As a result, we carried more spare parts than the average non-Europa cruiser that we met.

Rick anticipated the added maintenance requirements. He left his corporate position a year before we sailed and worked full-time commissioning boats for Bluewater Yachts, a Tayana dealership in New Rochelle, New York. After this he was able to commission *Sojourner* on his own, learning her systems from the bottom up. This experience paid for itself many times over.

Our only offshore experience prior to the circumnavigation was a round-trip passage to Bermuda in our Tayana 37 in 1989. Looking back, we probably spent more time preparing for those two 700-mile legs than we did preparing for some of the two-week passages that we have done since. We studied celestial navigation, and I got my ham license. Neither, as it turned out, were required during Europa; we relied on our GPS with satnav backups for navigation and the SSB marine bands for communication. We attended seminars on safety, first aid, engine repair, and weather forecasting. Most were valuable, especially those offered prior to the Caribbean 1500 Rally from Norfolk, Virginia, to the Virgin Islands in October 1990.

Once our adventure began, we made special efforts to stay in contact with friends and business associates, both for the emotional support of friends and relatives and for important business networking when we returned.

To handle our affairs at home, we hired the owner of an office-services business, Jayne, who was also a friend and interested in our travels. We used her address as our own and installed a separate phone line with an answering machine in her office. That gave us an AT&T credit card, which is usable in an amazing number of countries where USA direct-dial services are available. Via fax we could direct Jayne where to send mail or how to work out the logistics of our tax returns.

We had fun writing a newsletter (using my laptop and a simple dot-matrix printer) to record our impressions and adventures. We would send one copy of the newsletter and a printout of sticky-back labels to Jayne. She made copies, stuffed and labeled the envelopes, and sent the newsletter via U.S. mail. We constantly updated our mailing list, deleting and adding the names of friends, relatives, business associates, and people we met.

The way we handled our communications with the monthly phone and credit-card bills in New Jersey, newsletters ($75 to $100 every two or three months), and faxes (from $2 to $15 a page from every port) cost more than most cruisers would spend. However, we felt communication was key to our reentry to the working world when we elected to return.

Both Rick and I explored new ways to make a living during the voyage. I learned that I get a great deal of ego fulfillment from seeing my byline in print. I also faced the reality that after earning $2,685 in 1991 by writing, I was unlikely to be able to make a full-time living as a freelancer. We were surprised at how many conversations we had in the cockpits of boats that centered on what we and others would be doing when we returned. By and large, the owners of the boats in the Europa fleet were successful business people who acted as excellent sounding boards.

Midway in the voyage, we decided we would need to begin to plan our reentry with the same diligence that we planned our exit. We scheduled a trip back to the States at the end of the rally to decide whether we would return then or enjoy another year of cruising. We knew that if and when either one of us found an interesting opportunity, we would have to be flexible enough to jump at it. We knew our business contacts at home who had thought we were crazy to take off in the first place would carefully evaluate our "commitment to work again" before giving either of us an opportunity.

In the end our flexibility paid off. After the rally I had to fly back from the Mediterranean early to start a job in Massachusetts, while Rick brought the boat back with crew. Rick learned from the experience of being a skipper that running a boat on a schedule involves many of the same skills as running a small company. Now he is testing his skills by starting his own company. It's far different from his pre-cruising career as national sales manager for a pharmaceutical company.

Freshly back into our land lives, we often hear from our cruising friends. Many, like ourselves, are "ready" to return to land for a while. For Europa 92 travelers, that may be partly due to the added rigors that circumnavigating on a schedule entails. It may also reflect the weariness of always being a tourist in a changing array of countries. Some of our non-Europa cruising friends are going into the charter business to extend their time cruising. Others have established a seasonal cruising life, leaving their boat "on the hard" somewhere in the world during the local off-season. Then, of course, there are those friends who have passed into double-digit years of cruising and are still only an ocean or two into their circumnavigation. After our experience circumnavigating on a schedule, we think perhaps we'll follow their lead next time.

Just as cruisers are individuals, their styles of cruising are individualized. Most will argue that theirs is the best way to go. Ours, we can only claim, was the best way for us.

CONTRIBUTORS

LIZA COPELAND and her family recently circumnavigated aboard *Bagheera*. Look for her book *Still Cruising* and video "Just Cruising."

LAURA HACKER-DURBIN and husband Randy divide their cruising time between New Zealand and the tropical islands of the South Pacific.

BOB AND CAROL FARRINGTON sailed *Kitty Grace,* a Goderich 35, for ten years before moving ashore in Bequia, West Indies, where they operate a canvas shop. They have two daughters and nine grandchildren.

PAUL G. GILL, JR., is the author of *The Onboard Medical Handbook: First-Aid and Emergency Medicine Afloat.*

DAN HAUN logs sewing hours on rainy winter days but spends the rest of his free time sailing the Gulf of Mexico aboard his 27-foot sloop, *Akamai,* from his home in New Orleans.

DIANA JESSIE and her husband, Jim, have recently completed a five-year voyage around the North Pacific Rim, including China, Russia, Japan, and the Aleutians, with crew. Look for their video, "Be Your Own Sailboat Surveyor, Almost" and Diana's book, *A Woman's Guide to Cruising.*

JOHN KETTLEWELL cruises East Coast waters on his 32-foot catamaran, *Echo.* He is the author of an Intracoastal Waterway Chartbook.

JAY C. KNOLL cruises Caribbean and Florida waters.

BETH LEONARD completed an Atlantic circle during the 1990s, followed by a tropical circumnavigation aboard the Shanon 37 *Silk.* In the past few years she has cruised the higher latitudes, both North and South, aboard the custom sloop *Hawk.* She has written several books on sailing, including the highly acclaimed *Voyager's Handbook,* and numerous articles.

TOM LINSKEY was a senior editor at SAIL Magazine. He cruises New England aboard his J/32, *Independence.* He is the author of *Race-Winning Strategies.*

KATHY MIX and her husband, Dave, cruise on *Myth,* their self-designed and -built 55-foot ketch.

JULIE PALM and her husband, Rick, reside on the Eastern Shore of Maryland in Chesapeake Bay territory, and are currently boatless, but have taken up flying in the meantime. They hope to cruise again in the very near future once they have ceased to be worker bees.

LIN AND LARRY PARDEY continue to globetrot on *Taleisin,* their self-built 29-foot, 6-inch cutter. To keep up with their whereabouts, check out their homepage at www.paracay.com/cgi-bin/ws400.cgi.

STEVE SALMON AND TINA OLTON were convinced after a six-month voyage to the South Pacific in 1990 that they wanted to cruise full-time when they retired. So in 1993 they sold the house, bought a new Valiant 40, and sailed west. They've since covered about 38,000 miles and visited 54 countries.

RON SCOTT, an attorney, sails *Starship,* his Cabo Rico 38, in Galveston Bay and the Gulf of Mexico.

DONALD M. STREET, JR., has written numerous cruising guides and corrected many charts in his 30 years of Caribbean cruising.

KIM TAYLOR and wife Sally spent 10 years living aboard their 44-foot Bruce Roberts Norfolk yawl in Portsmouth, England, during which they cruised extensively in the North Atlantic and South Pacific oceans. Currently land-based in the Bay of Islands, New Zealand, Kim writes and supplies photographs for cruising magazines around the world. He is the author of the *1994 Pacific Storm Survey.*

ROBIN LUTZ TESTA and her husband, Serge, have recently completed a circumnavigation on their 60-foot steel sloop, *Encanto.*

PATIENCE WALES is Editor of SAIL Magazine. She began sailing as a young adult and spent four years circumnavigating the world with her boat partners aboard their 42-foot ketch. In the late 1980s she spent 13 months passage-making aboard their 51-foot cutter, *Boston Light.* With her three partners Wales has owned a total of six boats, the latest being a 53-foot cutter, also named *Boston Light.* She describes herself as a water rat.

TOM WOOD AND KATHY BARRON have been writing about living aboard, cruising, and upgrading boats for over 20 years. They currently live on *Sojourner,* a 40-foot motorsailer, the sixth boat they have rebuilt.

INDEX

U.S. pilot charts, 4–6
U.S. Postal Service, 165
Upgrade, 70, 77, 93
VHF, 49, 92–3, 168
Vanuatu, 181
Varnish(ed), 45–6, 54, 107, 122, 144
Vegetables, 134–8, 143
Ventilation, 40–1, 54, 56, 91, 100, 128, 134, 143
Vieques, 13
Visas, 107, 168
Visibility, 5, 18–20, 63, 90
Voice of America, 164
Voyaging, 4–5, 26, 173
Watch, 30, 92, 95, 96–100, 116, 122, 124
Water, 12–3, 15, 19–21, 40–2, 47, 49, 52–3, 56, 61, 64–66, 69, 72, 86, 91, 93, 102, 106, 119, 124–5, 127–30, 134, 136, 144, 147–52, 154, 156, 164, 168, 171
    blue, 88, 90–1, 111, 185
    choppy, 19
    coastal/U.S. territorial, 7, 168
    European, 7
    filters, 151–2
    floodwater, 103
    fresh, 42, 55, 118, 124–9, 138, 147, 149–51
    generator, 93
    hazards, 148
    jugs, 27, 30, 145
    local, 7, 118
    pumps, 48-9
    saltwater, 88, 106, 124, 127, 129, 149, 154
    slack, 21
    treating, 148
    tropical, 15
    waterline, 24, 64–5, 72
    watermaker, 49, 74, 124, 149
    waterproof/tight, 42–3, 56, 69, 119
Waypoint, 3, 11–2, 20–1, 26, 47, 90
Weather, 3–8, 23–4, 26, 19, 31, 37, 39–41, 47, 51, 55, 64–5, 71, 86, 89–90, 92–3, 105, 114, 118-20, 124, 134, 143, 162, 182, 184
    foul-weather gear, 39–41, 55, 119, 124

heavy, 26, 89, 182
inclement, 120
light, 23–4, 29
weather helm, 31
weather window, 162
weatherfax, 92, 171
windy, 71
Web commerce, 162
Web site, 163
Webbing, 37–8, 144
Whisker pole, 28–30
Wind, 23, 25, 27–31, 54–5, 61, 63–6, 71–2, 88–9, 91–3, 97–9, 102, 104, 106, 124, 127–8, 134, 149–50
    apparent, 27
    downwind, 27–30, 64, 89, 143
    generator, 55, 91–3, 149
    head-to-wind, 30
    high, 53, 61
    light, 24, 27, 30–1
    upwind, 30, 162
    vanes, 31, 88, 93
    velocity, 88
Windward, 25–7, 29, 62, 65, 70, 103, 143
Windbugger wind generator, 149
Windlass, 46–7, 61, 73–4, 86–7
Worldwide Marine Weather Forecasts, 8
Yacht, 39, 78–80, 102, 112–4, 130, 138, 156, 165, 184
    club, 102, 112, 114, 130, 138
    for hire, 113
Yawl, 12
Yemen, 23, 136